OUT
OF THE
MOUTHS
OF
BABES

OUT
OF THE
MOUTHS
OF
BABES

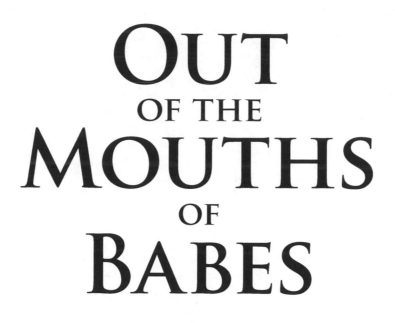

Songs and Poems about Me

DR. RENÉ BOYER

ARCHWAY
PUBLISHING

Archway Publishing books may be ordered through booksellers or by contacting:

Archway Publishing
1663 Liberty Drive
Bloomington, IN 47403
www.archwaypublishing.com
1 (888) 242-5904

ISBN: 978-1-4808-3483-5 (sc)
ISBN: 978-1-4808-3484-2 (e)

Library of Congress Control Number: 2016912450

Print information available on the last page.

Archway Publishing rev. date: 08/26/2016

What Is this Book About?

The early childhood years are so much fun. Children learn about themselves, who they are and what they are capable of doing. They learn about the world around them as they explore the natural elements of sun and rain, falling leaves and freshly fallen snowflakes.

Reading about and/or visiting a farm, zoo, or aquarium helps children learn about other living things in their world. By following daily routines, they learn the parts of their bodies and how to take care of them. By interacting with other children and family members, they learn about the importance of friendship, how to make and keep a friend.

Out of the Mouths of Babes provides a view of the child's world as it is expressed through song and poetry. While the lyrics of the songs reflect a contemporary view of the early childhood years, many of the melodies chosen are those already known and loved by people throughout our world. The song choices in this book are amazing! They reflect the America that children experience and are a part of today.

This book is especially handy for early childhood caregivers, teachers, parents, grandparents, and friends who want the attention and laughter from little ones, as they listen to their world and how they see themselves in it.

CONTENTS

My Smile

My smile goes with me everywhere
So all the world can see
How happy I am every day.
It's a gift I give for free.

Happy

Words and Music by Rene Boyer

I am hap - py, yes sir - ree! I am hap - py, can't you see?

I am hap - py, you'll a - gree, This great smile is part of me.

Good Morning Song

Words and Music by Rene Boyer

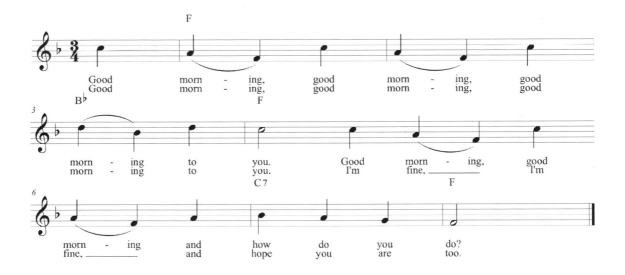

Good morn - ing, good morn - ing, good
Good morn - ing, good morn - ing, good

morn - ing to you. Good morn - ing, good
morn - ing to you. I'm fine, I'm

morn - ing and how do you do?
fine, and hope you are too.

CHILD AT PLAY

First I rise and brush my teeth.
Then I wash my face.
After breakfast, nice and hot,
I open my toy case.

I pull out all my dinosaurs,
My train, my cars, my cape.
I put my knight in his castle grand
Along with Lion and Ape.

I growl fiercely. I'm a lion
In a jungle green,
Prowling, scratching, roaring
While listening to monkeys scream!

I go outside and play a while.
I look at everything;
The rocks, the leaves, the sky so blue.
Then finally in my swing,
I push myself through wondrous worlds
Of pizza and ice cream.

Smile, Smile Smile!
Tune: In That Great Gitn' Up Morning

African American Spiritual
New Lyrics by Rene Boyer

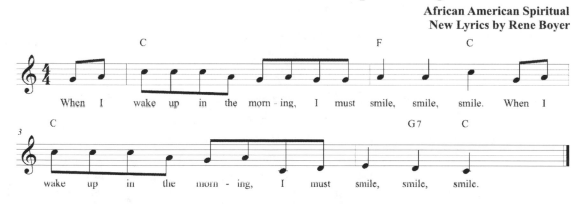

2. When I look into the mirror,
I must smile, smile, smile.
When I look into the mirror,
I must smile, smile smile.

3. When I finish eating breakfast,
I must smile and say, "Thank you."
When I finish eating breakfast,
I must smile and say, "Thank you."

4. When I see my friends at school,
I must smile and say, "Hi!"
When I see my friends at school,
I must smile and say, "Hi!"

5. When I leave to go back home,
I must smile and wave,"Goodbye!"
When I leave to go back home,
I must smile and wave, "Goodbye!"

These Are The Things We Do Every Day
Tune: Mulberry Bush

Traditional
New Lyrics by Boyer

These are the things we do ev'-ry day, we do ev'-ry day, we do ev'-ry day. These are the things we do ev'-ry day, so ear-ly in the morn - ing.

2. This is the way we wash our face.. .
3. This is the way we brush our teeth.. .
4. This is the way we put on our clothes. . .
5. This is the way we put on our shoes. . .
6. This is the way we comb our hair. . .
7. This is the way we play with our toys. .

My Days of the Week
Tune: Jack and Jill

Children's Song
New Words by Boyer

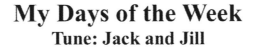

Sun - day, Mon - day, Tues - day, Wednes - day, Thurs day, Fri - day, Sat - ur-day. These are the days that make my week, and there can be no oth - er.

2. Everyday, I love to play,
With toys and my computer.
I go outdoors, I run, make noise,
Unless there's rain and thunder.

MY ROCKING HORSE

My rocking horse is awesome!
He takes me everywhere.
I just have to get on top,
So I climb up on my chair.

I close my eyes and imagine
Places I wish to see,
Like Dinosaur Island and Candy Land
And a pirate's ship at sea.

With reins in hand and feet in place
And a bag of carrot sticks,
I say the words, "Giddy-up, giddy-up!"
Then, away we go on our trip!

Sometimes I make him go so fast,
It really tires me out.
But once there, I can truly say,
"It was worth it, without a doubt."

I feed my horse bananas,
Sometimes potato chips,
If I have my bottle,
I'll give him a generous sip.

Regardless of what I feed him,
There's always a great big mess.
I really don't think he's hungry.
Perhaps he wanted less?

Rocking Horse and I both know
That there's a lot to see.
"But your time to see is limited,"
Said Rocking Horse to me.

Rocking Horse Song
Tune: Mary Had A Little Lamb

Words by Boyer

2. My horse loves to trot, trot trot,
Trot, trot, trot, trot, trot trot,
My horse loves to trot, trot, trot,
Each and every day.

3. My horse tells me, "Neigh, neigh!"
"Neigh, neigh!", "Neigh, neigh!"
My horse tells me, "Neigh, neigh!"
When he wants some hay.

4. He decides to stop, stop, stop,
Stop, stop, stop, stop, stop, stop.
He decides to stop, stop, stop,
If I don't obey.

5. Horsey Dear, "Here is some hay,
Is some hay, Is some hay,
Horsey dear, here is some hay,
Eat, you'll be okay."

6. Now, we can be on our way,
On our way, on our way,
Now we can be on our way,
There's lots to do today.

The Grand Old Duke of York

Traditional

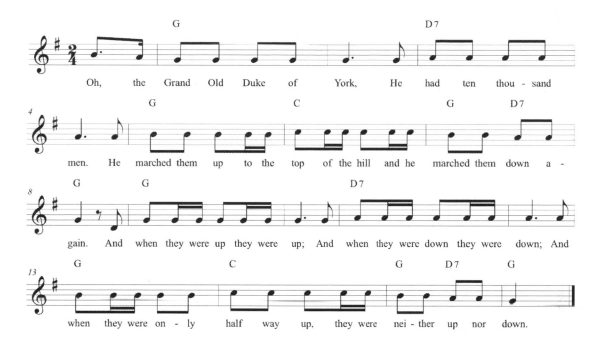

Oh, the Grand Old Duke of York, He had ten thou - sand men. He marched them up to the top of the hill and he marched them down a - gain. And when they were up they were up; And when they were down they were down; And when they were on - ly half way up, they were nei - ther up nor down.

She'll Be Coming Round the Mountain

American Folk Song

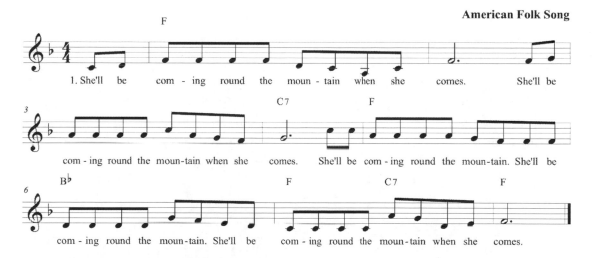

1. She'll be com - ing round the moun - tain when she comes. She'll be com - ing round the moun - tain when she comes. She'll be com - ing round the moun - tain. She'll be com - ing round the moun - tain. She'll be com - ing round the moun - tain when she comes.

2. She'll be driving six white horses when she comes . . .
3. She'll be coming down a road that's five miles long . . .
4. We will all go out to meet her when she comes . . .
5. We will all have chicken and dumplings when she comes . . .

MY BODY

My nose and ears sit on my face,
Accompanied by two eyes.
They help me to protect myself
So I won't be surprised.

My nose helps me to smell things.
My ears help me to hear.
My eyes help me to see my world.
They make it very clear.

My mouth is not so little.
It houses teeth and tongue.
Together with my little lips,
I blow up bubblegum.

I also use my mouth, you know,
To speak and sing nice tunes,
Like "Twinkle, Twinkle, Little Star"
And "By the Light of the Silvery Moon."

My throat provides a pathway
For all my food to go
Into my tiny tummy
So I can grow and grow.

My shoulders are important.
They help to hold my clothes
On my tiny body
So I won't get too cold.

My arms don't simply dangle
And swing back to and fro.
They help me reach above my head
And touch the ground below.

My fingers help me hold things.
I have exactly ten.
Five of them are on each hand
To hold my crayons in.

My waist is in my middle,
Allowing me to bend low.
My hips are slightly lower
To rest my hands just so.

My belly button's my center,
The very core of me.
It's here I was hooked to Mommy
When I was born, you see.

My thighs and legs are both attached
By a joint we call the knee
That helps me crawl, walk, and jump,
To move successfully.

My feet are very special.
They help me stand up tall.
Each foot has five toes on it
To kick my soccer ball.

My head is placed on very straight
But looks around to see
Anything and everything
That is a part of me.

Where Is Thumpkin?
Tune: Are You Sleeping?

American Folk Song

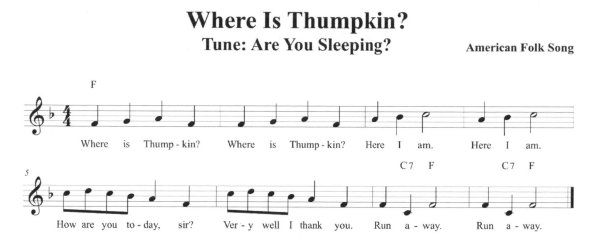

Verses: 2. Where is Pointer? . . . 3. Where is Tall Man? . . . 4. Where is Ring Man? . . . 5. Where is Pinky? . .

Head, Shoulders, Knees and Toes

Traditional

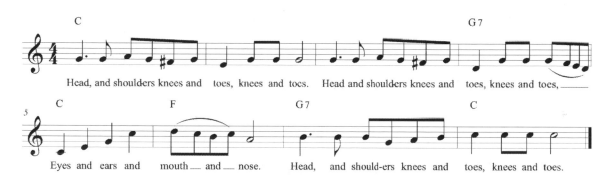

Clap Your Hands
Adapted Tune: John Brown Had A Little Indian

Lyrics by Rene Boyer

Juanito
(Little Johnny)

Children's Song from Spain

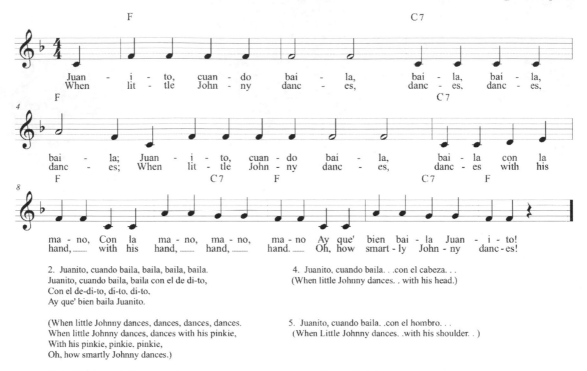

Juan - i - to, cuan - do bai - la, bai - la, bai - la,
When lit - tle John - ny danc - es, danc - es, danc - es,

bai - la; Juan - i - to, cuan - do bai - la, bai - la con la
danc - es; When lit - tle John - ny danc - es, danc - es with his

ma - no, Con la ma - no, ma - no, ma - no Ay que' bien bai - la Juan - i - to!
hand, with his hand, hand, hand. Oh, how smart - ly John - ny danc - es!

2. Juanito, cuando baila, baila, baila, baila.
Juanito, cuando baila, baila con el de di-to,
Con el de-di-to, di-to, di-to,
Ay que' bien baila Juanito.

(When little Johnny dances, dances, dances, dances.
When little Johnny dances, dances with his pinkie,
With his pinkie, pinkie. pinkie,
Oh, how smartly Johnny dances.)

3. Juanito, cuando baila. . . . con el pie. . .
(When little Johnny dances. . .with his foot. .)

4. Juanito, cuando baila. . .con el cabeza. . .
(When little Johnny dances. . with his head.)

5. Juanito, cuando baila. .con el hombro. . .
(When Little Johnny dances. .with his shoulder. .)

6. Juanito, cuando baila. . .con el codo. . .
(When little Johnny dances. . with his elbow.)

Open, Shut Them

Children's Hand Game

1. O - pen, shut them, o - pen, shut them, Give a lit - tle clap!
2. Creep them, creep them, creep them, creep them, Right up to your chin!
3. Shake them, shake them, shake them, shake them, Shake them just like this!

O - pen, shut them, o - pen, shut them, Lay them in your lap!
O - pen wide your lit - tle mouth, but do not put them in!
Roll them, roll them, roll them, roll them, Blow a lit - tle kiss!

Do Your Ears Hang Low?

Traditional

3. Do your ears hang wide?
Do they flip from side to side?
Do they wave in the breeze,
From the slightest little sneeze?
Can you soar above the nation,
With a feeling of elevation?
Do your ears hang wide?

4. Do your ears fall off,
When you give a great big cough?
Do they lie there on the ground,
Bounce up at every sound?
Can you stick them in your pocket,
Just like Davy Crockett?
Do your ears fall off?

5. Does your tongue hang down?
Does it flop all around?
Can you tie it in a knot?
Can you tie it in a bow?
Can you throw it o'er your shoulder
Like a Continental soldier?
Does your tongue hang down?

6. Does your nose hang low?
Does it wiggle to and fro?
Can you tie it in a knot?
Can you tie it in a bow?
Can you throw it o'er your shoulder,
Like a Continenttal soldier?
Does you nose hang low?

7. Do your eyes pop out?
Do they bounce all about?
Can you tie them in a knot?
Can you tie them in a bow?
Can you throw them o'er your shoulder,
Like a Continental shoulder?
Do your eyes pop out?

MACARONI AND CHEESE

Spaghetti and pizza are all I'll eat!
On this I must insist!
Perhaps a banana or apple
Might be added to my list.

Oatmeal is good, and pancakes too,
When served up nice and hot,
But soft-boiled eggs, shredded wheat—
Absolutely not!

I won't eat green, no matter what!
If I see it, I will cry.
But if it is well hidden,
I might give it a try.

I'll always tell you, "Thank you,"
And remember to say "please,"
As long as I can always have
Macaroni and cheese!

Short'nin' Bread

Plantation Song
Arranged by Rene Boyer

Put on the skil-let,......... Put on the pan, Ma-ma's gon-na make a lit-tle short-'nin' bread.

That's not all she's go-ing to do, Ma-ma's going to make a lit-tle choc' late too.

Ma-ma's lit-tle ba-by loves short-'nin, short-'nin, Ma-ma's lit-tle ba-by loves short-'nin bread.

Ma-ma's lit-tle ba-by loves short-'nin, short-'nin, Ma-ma's lit-tle ba-by loves short-'nin bread.

The Muffin Man

English Folk Song
Arranged by Rene Boyer

Oh, do you know the muf - fin man, the muf - fin man, the muf - fin man? Oh, do you know the muf - fin man, who lives on Dru - ry Lane?

Other Verses: Oh, do you know the pancake man. . the bagel man. . .the ice cream man. . . the barbecue man, etc.

I Want to Eat

Music and Lyrics by Rene Boyer

1. I want to eat an ap - ple, ap - ple,
2. I want to eat an o - range, o - range,

ap - ple, I want to eat an ap - ple, ev' - er - y Mon - day.
o - range, I want to eat an o - range, ev' - er - y Tues - day.

3. I want to eat bananas. . . .every Wednesday.
4. I want to eat some peaches. . every Thursday.
5. I want to eat some melon. . . every Friday.
6. I want to eat some berries . . .every Saturday.
7. I want to eat tomatoes. . .every Sunday.

BROWNIES

One, two, three, __
Four, five, six. __
Stir, stir, stir the
Brownie mix.

Add three eggs, __
Water, too. __
Add some nuts
If it suits you.

One, two, three, __
Four, five, six. __
Batter's ready.
Want to lick?

Put it in the pan,
Bake it till it's done.
When they're ready,
Do you want one?

I'm A Little Tea Pot

George Harry Sanders
Clarence Kelly

I'm a lit-tle tea-pot, short and stout. Here is my han-dle, here is my spout.

When I get all steamed up, hear me shout. Tip, me o-ver and pour me out!

Arroz Con Leche

Spanish Lullaby

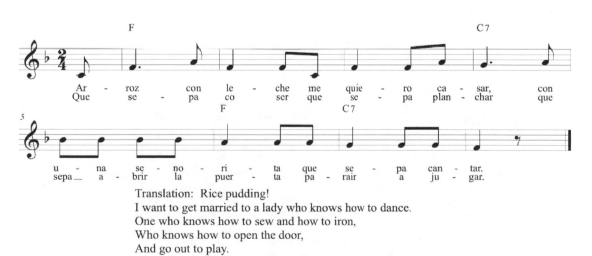

Ar - roz con le - che me quie - ro ca - sar, con
Que se - pa co ser que se - pa plan - char, que

u - na se - no - ri - ta que se - pa can - tar.
sepa a - brir la puer - ta pa - rair a ju - gar.

Translation: Rice pudding!
I want to get married to a lady who knows how to dance.
One who knows how to sew and how to iron,
Who knows how to open the door,
And go out to play.

Bate Bate

Mexican Folk Song

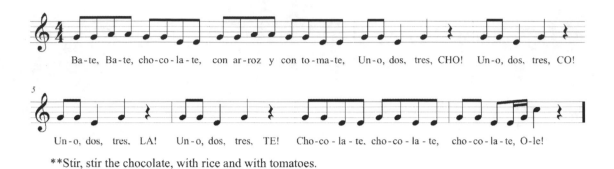

Ba - te, Ba - te, cho - co - la - te, con ar - roz y con to - ma - te, Un - o, dos, tres, CHO! Un - o, dos, tres, CO!

Un - o, dos, tres, LA! Un - o, dos, tres, TE! Cho - co - la - te, cho - co - la - te, cho - co - la - te, O - le!

**Stir, stir the chocolate, with rice and with tomatoes.

Sing a Song of Sixpense

Traditional

E♭   B♭   B♭9

Sing   a song   of six - pense,   a poc - ket full   of rye.

E♭

Four   and twen - ty black - birds,   baked   in   a pie.

B♭   B♭9

When   the pie   was o - pened,   the birds be - gan   to sing.

D dim

Was' - nt that   a dain - ty dish   to set   be - fore   the King.   (The)

2. The King was in his counting house, counting all his money.
The Queen was in the parlor, eating bread and honey.
The maid was in the garden, hanging up the clothes, when
Out jumped a blackbird, and pecked off her nose.

IN THE TUB

Splish, splash, splish, splash!
Finally, I'm in the tub,
In water prepared just for me
So I can scrub-a-dub-dub.

The soap is oh so slippery!
It's hard to hold onto.
It dives into the water
And disappears from view.

My rubber ducky loves it!
He goes right with the flow,
Exploring different places.
"Now, where did Ducky go?"

Splish, splash, splish, splash!
I love it—yes, I do.
From head to toe, I wash just so.
Now, I feel brand-new.

Rubber Duckie
Tune: Hot Cross Buns

New Lyrics by Boyer

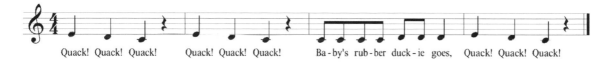

Quack! Quack! Quack! Quack! Quack! Quack! Ba-by's rub-ber duck-ie goes, Quack! Quack! Quack!

Pin Pon

Latin American Folk Song

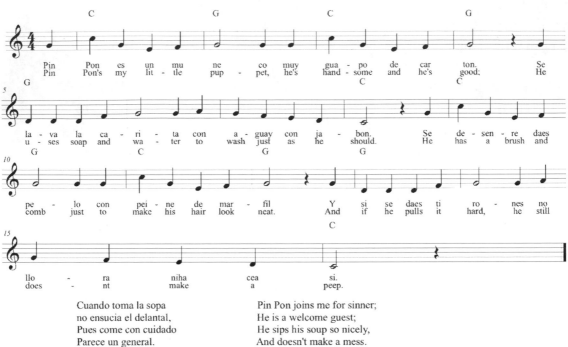

Pin Pon es un mu ne co muy gua po de car ton. Se
Pin Pon's my lit tle pup pet, he's hand some and he's good; He

la va la ca ri ta con a guay con ja bon. Se de sen re daes
u ses soap and wa ter to wash just as he should. He has a brush and

pe lo con pei ne de mar fil Y si se daes ti ro nes no
comb just to make his hair look neat. And if he pulls it hard, he still

llo ra niha cea si.
does nt make a peep.

Cuando toma la sopa
no ensucia el delantal,
Pues come con cuidado
Parece un general.
Y cuando las estrellas
empiczan a brillar,
Pin Pon se va a la cama
se a cuesta a descansar.

Pin Pon joins me for sinner;
He is a welcome guest;
He sips his soup so nicely,
And doesn't make a mess.
When night time comes upon us,
And stars are twinkling bright,
Pin Pon gets in his bed,
And I hear him say "Good Night."

Pito Pito

Spanish Game Song

Pi to, Pi to co lo ri to, Don de vas tu, tan bon i to.
Pi to Pi to, You're so color ful Where're you go ing looking so cute!

Al a cer a ver da der a, Ping, Pong, Fue ra!
I am go ing some place spe cial, Ping, Pong, Out!

POTTY TIME

There's comfort in wearing a diaper.
You don't worry about a thing.
Someone comes to change you—
Suddenly you're nice and clean.

But now I think it's over,
At least as I've been told;
I'm expected to go and sit each day
On a toilet bowl.

The potty is really big, you know.
I'm scared that I'll fall in.
But I have a special step stool
And a seat for my rear end.

I try to use the step stool
To get up to the top,
But it's difficult to manage,
So sometimes I have to squat.

Once up, it's not too easy
To pull my undies down,
So I must have a helper
To be instantly around.

I'm supposed to shout out, "Potty!"
When it's time to go,
But I can't always do that—
I have a life, you know.

I get so tied up with my toys
Or with my favorite show
That sometimes I simply do forget
That I really need to go.

One day soon, I'll be able
To go potty on my own.
Meanwhile, please don't rush me,
And for goodness sake, don't groan!

We're Going to the Potty

Words and Music by Rene Boyer

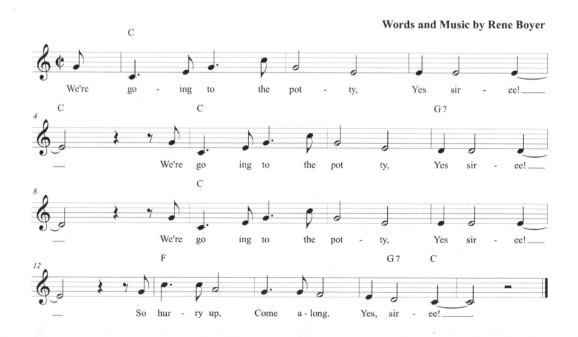

We're go-ing to the pot-ty, Yes sir-ee!

We're go ing to the pot ty, Yes sir - ee!

We're go ing to the pot-ty, Yes sir - ee!

So hur-ry up, Come a-long. Yes, sir - ee!

DAYCARE

I'm still a baby. Can't they see?
What makes them act this way,
To suddenly just drop me off
With strangers for a day?

I do not like it, not one bit!
I want to go back home.
I'll scream and cry, and they will see
That this is surely wrong.

A lady tries to calm me down
By gently rubbing my back.
I don't care: I'm all enraged.
But when she offers me a snack,

My tears dry up, and then a smile
Creeps across my face.
Perhaps I can begin to spend
An hour in this place.

Hush Little Baby

American Folk Song

1. Hush lit-tle ba-by, don't say a word. Pa-pa's gon-na buy you a mock-ing bird,
If that mock-ing bird don't sing, Pa-pa's gon-na buy you a dia-mond ring.

2. And if that diamond ring turns to brass,
Papa's gonna buy you a looking glass.
And if that looking glass gets broke,
Papa's gonna buy you a billy goat.

3. And if that billy goat won't pull,
Papa's gonna buy you a cart and bull.
And it that cart and bull turn over,
Papa's gonna buy you a dog named Rover.

4. And if that dog named Rover won't bark,
Papa's gonna buy you a horse and cart.
And if that horse and cart fall down,
You're still the sweetest little baby in town.

Little Johnny Brown

A traditional play party-game
from the Georgia Sea Islands.

African-American Folk Song

Lit - tle John - ny Brown,_____ Lay your com - fort down._____

Lit - tle John - ny Brown,_____ Lay your com - fort down._____

Fold one cor - ner John-ny_____ Brown. Fold a-noth-er cor - ner John-ny_____ Brown.

Fold a-noth-er cor - ner John-ny_____ Brown. Fold a-noth-er cor - ner John-ny_____ Brown.

Show them your stuff now, John-ny_____ Brown, Show them your stuff now John-ny_____ Brown.

Give it to a-noth - er John-ny_____ Brown, Give it to a-noth - er John-ny_____ Brown.

MY PLAY DATE

If you are a little kid
And want to be really cool,
You should have a play date
With a favorite friend from school.

It doesn't matter where you meet.
It's always lots of fun!
Sharing toys and laughter
Away from everyone.

A grown-up will provide a lunch
Or maybe just a snack.
It all depends on when you start
And when you're expected back.

I so enjoy a play date
With my special friend.
It makes me feel so happy.
I never want it to end.

See See My Playmate

Children's Game Song
Rene Boyer Version

See see my play-mate, come out and play with me, and bring your dol-lies three, climb up my ap-ple tree, Slide down my rain-bow, in-to my cel-lar door, and we'll be jol-ly friends, for-ev-er more, more, shut the door!

Clean-Up Time!
Tune: Hot Cross Buns

Traditional
New Lyrics by Boyer

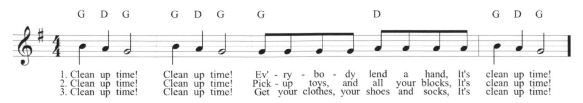

1. Clean up time! Clean up time! Ev'-ry-bo-dy lend a hand, It's clean up time!
2. Clean up time! Clean up time! Pick-up toys, and all your blocks, It's clean up time!
3. Clean up time! Clean up time! Get your clothes, your shoes and socks, It's clean up time!

THE LOST MITTEN

Every time I go to play,
My mitten seems to run away.
It's not in my pocket and not in my sleeve.
Another lost mitten, can you believe?

Three Little Kittens

Traditional

Three lit - tle kit - tens have lost their mit - tens, and they be - gan to cry.

Moth - er dear, we sad - ly fear that we have lost our mit - tens _____

"Lost your mit - tens, You naugh - ty kit - tens, then you shall have no pie!"

"Meow, meow, meow, meow, now we shall have no pie!"

2. "Mother dear, see here, see here,
   We have found our mittens."
   "Put on your mittens, you silly kittens
   And you shall have some pie."
   "Meow, meow, meow, meow!
   Now we shall have some pie!"

FALLING

Yes, I love to fall,
And no, I won't get hurt.
The only thing that bothers me
Is a little bit of dirt.
But then again, why should I care?

I'm too small to clean
My clothes, my socks,
My coat and hat.
What do you think of that?

Ring Around the Rosie

Traditional

Ring a - round the ros - ie, a pock - et full of po - sies;
ash - es, ash - es, we all fall down.

Jack and Jill

Traditional

Jack and Jill went up the hill to fetch a pail of wa - ter.
Jack fell down and broke his crown, and Jill came tum - bl' - ing af - ter.

Jazzy Humpty

Boyer

1. Hump - ty Dump - ty was good look - in' ___ Hump - ty Dump - ty had it all. ___
2. All the King's men tried to help him, ___ There was lit - tle they could do. ___
3. There's a les - son we should learn here. ___ There is some - thing you should know. ___

Hump - ty Dump - ty tried to text me, ___ then ol' Hump - ty had a fall!
Tried to put him back to - geth - er, ___ us - ing dif - 'rent kinds of glue.
Stop the text - ing when you're walk - ing, ___ or you'll fall deep down be - low.

London Bridge is Falling Down

Traditional

C   G   C
Lon - don Bridge is fall - ing down, fall - ing down, fall - ing down.

                                     G   C
Lon - don Bridge is fall - ing down, my fair la - dy.

THE SANDBOX

The sandbox is my favorite place
To dream, to work, to play.
I scoop, shape, and build things
In a most creative way.

I literally spend hours
Loading my big dump truck,
Pushing it across the sand
And keeping it from getting stuck.

The sand helps me grow stronger
As I press it with my hands.
It helps me learn to measure
When filling my bucket and pan.

The only problem with it
Is when I go back home.
My socks and shoes are filled with it,
And my hair needs a brush and comb.

Sand ends up in places
That put grown-ups to a test,
But it doesn't bother me at all.
Sand is still the best!

My Sandy Land
Tune: Sandyland

**Georgia Folk Song
Words by Boyer**

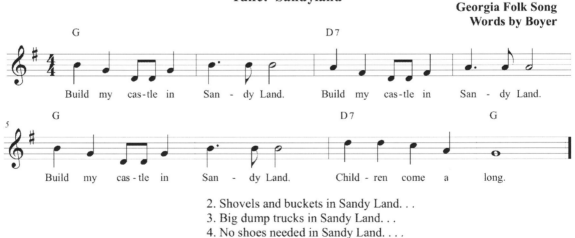

2. Shovels and buckets in Sandy Land. . .
3. Big dump trucks in Sandy Land. . .
4. No shoes needed in Sandy Land. . . .
5. Lots of fun in Sandy Land. . .

ZIP, BUTTON, SNAP

Zip, button, snap!
Zip, button, snap!
Little fingers have to learn to
Zip, button, snap!

Zip, button, snap!
Zip, button, snap!
If I want to dress myself, I
Zip, button, snap!

Zip, Button, Snap
Tune: This Little Light O Mine

Lyrics by Avis B. Christiansen
Tune by Harry Dixon Loes
New Lyrics by Boyer

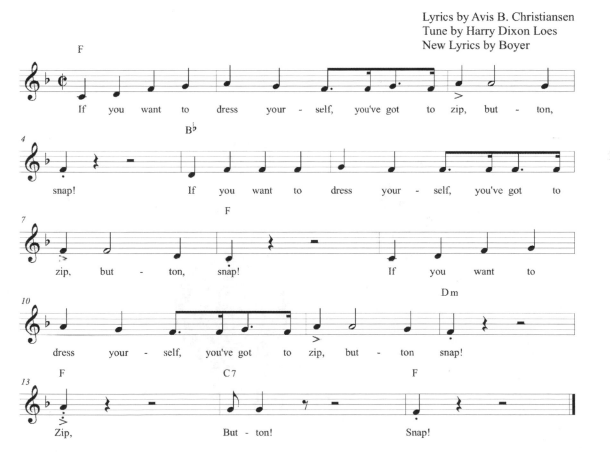

Miss Mary Mack

Children's Hand-Clapping Game

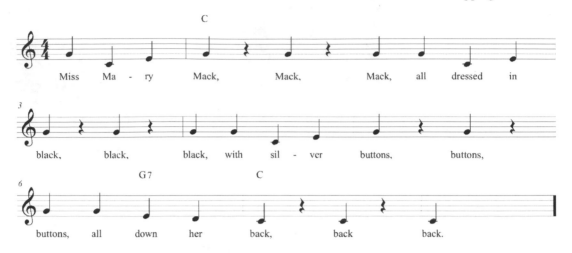

Miss Ma - ry Mack, Mack, Mack, all dressed in

black, black, black, with sil - ver buttons, buttons,

buttons, all down her back, back back.

2. She asked her mother, mother, mother,
   For fifty cents, cents, cents,
   To see the elephant, elephant, elephant,
   Jump the fence, fence, fence.

3. He jumped so high, high, high,
   'Til he reached the sky, sky, sky,
   And he didn't come back, back, back,
   'Til the Fourth of Ju-ly, -ly,-ly.

Looby Loo

Singing Game

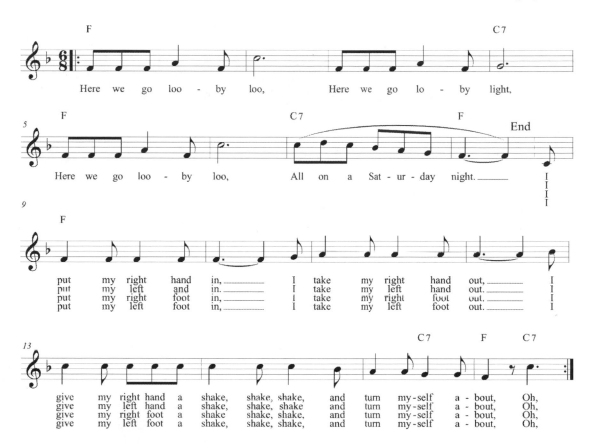

Here we go loo - by loo, Here we go lo - by light,

Here we go loo - by loo, All on a Sat - ur - day night.

put my right hand in,   I take my right hand out, I
put my left and in,   I take my left hand out, I
put my right foot in,   I take my right foot out, I
put my left foot in,   I take my left foot out, I

give my right hand a shake, shake, shake, and turn my-self a - bout, Oh,
give my left hand a shake, shake, shake and turn my-self a - bout, Oh,
give my right foot a shake, shake, shake, and turn my-self a - bout, Oh,
give my left foot a shake, shake, shake, and turn my-self a - bout, Oh,

WHICH SHALL I CHOOSE?

I have a major question
When putting on my shoes:
Left foot, right foot,
Which shall I choose?

To me it's like a puzzle
Whose parts don't seem to fit.
No matter how many times I try,
I make a mess of it.

"Your shoes are on the wrong feet!"
Is what I hear each day.
Honestly, I ask myself,
"Why can't they stay that way?"

Perhaps an arrow placed on each
Would help me correctly choose
Which shoe goes on which foot?
Then I won't be confused.

Did You Ever See A Lassie

Children's Song

Did you ev - er see a las - sie go this way and that way? Did you ev - er see a
Did you ev - er see a lad - die go this way and that way? did you ev - er see a

las - sie go this way and that? Go this way and that way, go this way and
lad - die go this way and that? Go this way and that way, go this way and

that way, Did you ev - er see a las - sie go this way and that?
that way, Did you ev - er see a lad - die go this way and that?

SHOELACES

It's tough buying a pair of shoes
When you can't tie a bow.
Why would a kid even want to learn?
Why not stick with Velcro?

That aside, it's important to know
How to do this special task.
So here am I to tell you.
You don't even have to ask.

First take a shoelace in each hand
And hold them up like so.
Crisscross and exchange them.
Now you're ready to go.

Use your thumpkin and pointer
To hold on to the string.
Try not think about it;
Let these fingers do their thing.

Pass one string over the other.
Take it under then pull it through.
Pull, pull, pull until both strings
Touch the top of your shoe.

Now it's time for fun and games.
Let go of your shoelace.
Pick one up, make a bunny ear,
Now hold that ear in place.

Take the other string and circle it
Around the bunny ear loop.
You'll see a little window,
Which you can pull another ear through.

Now you have two bunny ears,
Perfectly in place.
You can pull on each of them.
Hurrah, you've tied your lace!

Tie Your Shoe!
Tune: Taps

Traditional
Words: Boyer

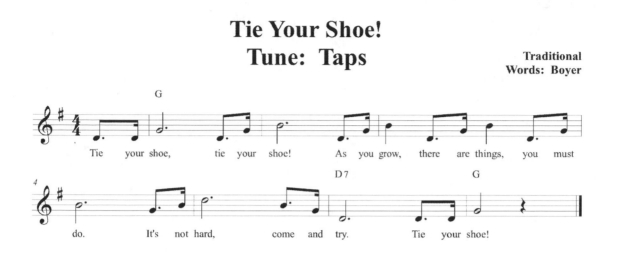

Tie your shoe, tie your shoe! As you grow, there are things, you must do. It's not hard, come and try. Tie your shoe!

One, Two, Tie My Shoe

Children's Counting Song

One, two, tie my shoe, Three, four, shut the door, Five, six, pick up sticks, Seven, eight, lay them straight, Nine, ten, a big fat hen.

MY BOOK BAG

My book bag is so special.
It carries many things.
My toys, my snack, and clothing
In case I need a change.

It mustn't be too heavy,
Or it will weigh me down.
Indeed I feel so happy
As I carry it around.

My Book Bag Song
Tune: Alouetta

French-Canadian Folksong
New Lyrics by Boyer

I have a book bag, a ve-ry spe-cial book bag. I have a book bag, I

car-ry-to school with me. My work goes in my book bag, my ve-ry spe-cial book bag, My

work goes in my book bag for ev' ry one to see.

MY YELLOW SCHOOL BUS

My yellow bus is awesome.
It rolls up hills and down.
It carries all the girls and boys
To schools throughout our town.

Doors open wide to let me in.
I always say, "Hello."
I climb up steps, then take my seat,
Buckle up, and I'm ready to go.

Through my window I see things:
Cars and commuter trains,
Fields of corn, trees and lakes
And horses with long black manes.

I see the snow in winter.
I see the flowers in spring.
I see blue skies in summer
Darken when it's going to rain.

I watch the leaves of autumn
Change from green to brown.
Some orange, red, and yellow
Gently flutter down.

There are many shapes and colors
I see along the way
While riding in my school bus.
It's a great way to start my day.

The Wheels on the Bus

Children's Song

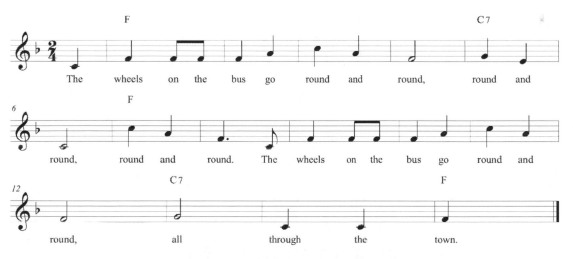

The wheels on the bus go round and round, round and round, round and round. The wheels on the bus go round and round, all through the town.

2. The wipers on the bus go swish, swish, swish. ...
3. The horn on the bus goes beep, beep, beep. . .
4. The people on the bus go up and down.. .
5. The babies on the bus go, "Wah, wah, wah!" . .
6. The doors on the bus go open and shut.
7. The driver on the bus goes, "Move on back!" . . .

A-Riding We Will Go
Tune: A-Hunting We Will Go

English Folk Song
New Lyrics by Rene Boyer

Oh, a - rid - ing we will go, a - rid - ing we will go, I'll
sit down next to Gus, in - side the yel - low bus, and then be read - y to go.

TRICYCLES, SCOOTERS, AND CARS

Tricycles, scooters, and cars!
These are the things I ride.
Whirling around while on the ground
With my helmet on.

Tricycles, scooters, and cars!
How much I do enjoy!
I pedal, push, glide, and steer,
Perfect for girls and boys.

Riding in My Stroller
Tune: Riding in My Buggy Miss Mary Jane

Play-Party Song
New Lyrics by Boyer

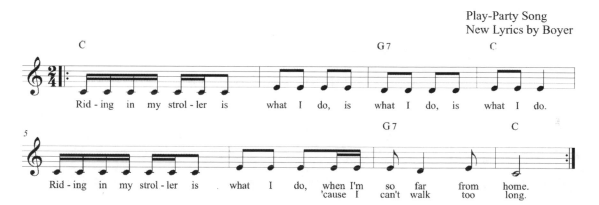

Rid-ing in my strol-ler is what I do, is what I do, is what I do.

Rid-ing in my strol-ler is what I do, when I'm so far from home.
'cause I can't walk too long.

MY SEATBELT

Although it's supposed to help me
In case of an accident,
I've problems with my seatbelt,
And I feel I need to vent.

Most adults who strap me in
Don't know what to do.
If I were not fully dressed,
I'd be black and blue.

They pull my poor arms back and forth.
They try to be polite,
But they sometimes forget my size
And strap me in too tight.

Once settled in my car seat,
I sometimes take a nap.
It's a good thing that I'm flexible
'Cause my head falls on my lap.

One day when I can really speak,
I'll tell them a thing or two.
"I want you to fasten my seatbelt,
But first please think it through!"

Down By the Station
Tune: Adapted from Alouette

Traditional French

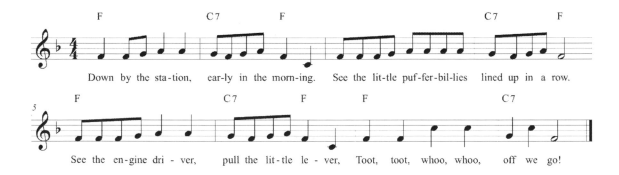

Down by the sta-tion, ear-ly in the morn-ing. See the lit-tle puf-fer-bil-lies lined up in a row. See the en-gine dri-ver, pull the lit-tle le-ver, Toot, toot, whoo, whoo, off we go!

THE TRAIN!

Toot! Toot!
Chug-a-chug-a, chug-a-chug-a—
Toot! Toot!
Here comes the train!

Toot! Toot!
Chug-a-chug-a, chug-a-chug-a—
Oh no!
It's going to rain!

Toot! Toot!
Chug-a-chug-a, chug-a-chug-a—
Toot! Toot!
Oh, what a shame!

Toot! Toot!
Chug-a-chug-a, chug-a-chug-a—
"Hi, Mom!"
"You're home again."

This Train

Spiritual
Arr. Rene Boyer

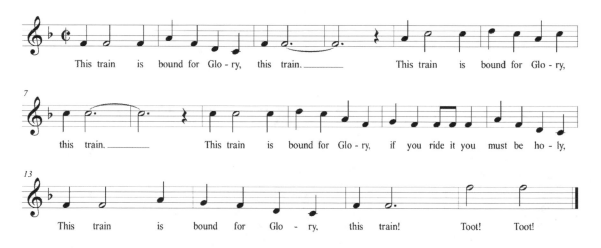

This train is bound for Glo-ry, this train._____ This train is bound for Glo-ry,

this train._____ This train is bound for Glo-ry, if you ride it you must be ho-ly,

This train is bound for Glo-ry, this train! Toot! Toot!

Get On Board

African American Spiritual

Get on board, lit - tle chil - dren. Get on board, lit - tle

chil - dren. Get on board, lit - tle chil - dren, there's room for man - y a

Fine

more. The gos - pel train's a - com - ing, I hear it close at

D.C. al Fine

hand. ___ I hear the car-wheels rum-bling and trav - ling through this land,

Chug-A-Chug-A Toot Toot!

Tune: Skip to My Lou

Melody Adapted by Rene Boyer
New Lyrics by Rene Boyer

Chug - a - chug - a toot, toot, red ca - boose, Chug - a - chug - a toot, toot, red ca - boose.

Chug - a - chug - a toot, toot, red ca - boose. Rol - ling down the track past me and you.

A Pirate Ship
Tune: I Saw Three Ships

Traditional
New Lyrics by Boyer

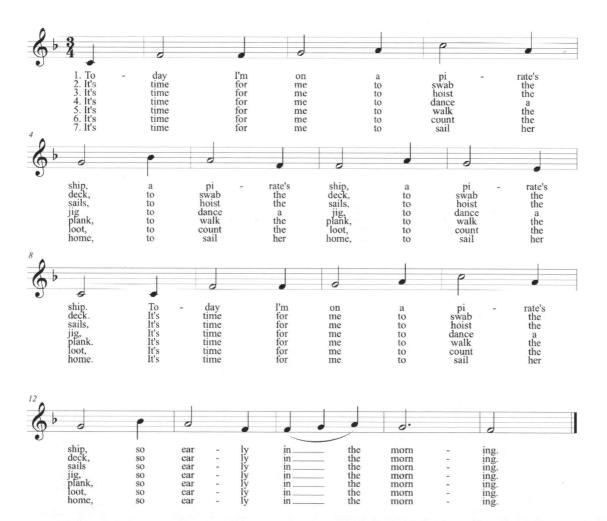

1. To - day   I'm   on   a   pi - rate's
2. It's time   for   me   to   swab   the
3. It's time   for   me   to   hoist   the
4. It's time   for   me   to   dance   a
5. It's time   for   me   to   walk   the
6. It's time   for   me   to   count   the
7. It's time   for   me   to   sail   her

ship,   a   pi - rate's   ship,   a   pi - rate's
deck,   to   swab   the   deck,   to   swab   the
sails,   to   hoist   the   sails,   to   hoist   the
jig,   to   dance   a   jig,   to   dance   a
plank,   to   walk   the   plank,   to   walk   the
loot,   to   count   the   loot,   to   count   the
home,   to   sail   her   home,   to   sail   her

ship.   To - day   I'm   on   a   pi - rate's
deck.   It's   time   for   me   to   swab   the
sails,   It's   time   for   me   to   hoist   the
jig,   It's   time   for   me   to   dance   a
plank.   It's   time   for   me   to   walk   the
loot,   It's   time   for   me   to   count   the
home.   It's   time   for   me   to   sail   her

ship,   so   ear - ly   in ____ the   morn - ing.
deck,   so   ear - ly   in ____ the   morn - ing.
sails   so   ear - ly   in ____ the   morn - ing.
jig,   so   ear - ly   in ____ the   morn - ing.
plank,   so   ear - ly   in ____ the   morn - ing.
loot,   so   ear - ly   in ____ the   morn - ing.
home,   so   ear - ly   in ____ the   morn - ing.

CARTOON FUN

Cartoon day is every day,
At least an hour or two.
I don't think that everyone
Likes this point of view.

But trust me when I tell you.
I learn so many things
About the world around me
And the knowledge that it brings.

I learn of paleontology,
Chemistry, and biology too.
I learn about astronomy
And that pandas eat bamboo.

I've learned another language.
I visit many lands.
I know the most important days
In Mexico and Japan.

I've learned to count, to sound out words
And sing some special songs.
I've learned to follow directions
And not do others wrong.

Cartoons are most helpful,
And to me, it is my way
To learn and still have lots of fun,
Day after day after day.

Cartoon Fun Song
Tune: Great Big House in New Orleans

Louisiana Folk Song
New Lyrics by Boyer

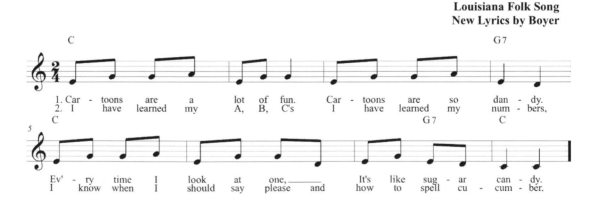

1. Car - toons are a lot of fun. Car - toons are so dan - dy.
2. I have learned my A, B, C's I have learned my num - bers,

Ev' - ry time I look at one, It's like sug - ar can - dy.
I know when I should say please and how to spell cu - cum - ber.

READING

Do you know that I memorize
Every book you read?
Whether it's about a falling star
Or a pumpkin seed?

I listen to everything you say.
I look at pictures too.
My mind is like a great big sponge,
Unlimited in what it can do.

I caution you to slow down.
I want to hear every word.
It doesn't do me any good
If what you read is blurred.

Don't worry if I ask you,
"Please, please read it again."
I'm simply in the process
Of taking it all in.

Reading is a wonder!
It allows me to take trips,
To visit any and every place.
I can take my pick.

I love for you to read to me.
I hope you now know why.
I long to read well, just like you,
And I will. Let me try.

Read, Read, Read!
Tune: Three Blind Mice

Traditional
New Lyrics by Rene Boyer

Read, read, read! Read, read, read! Read a-bout the di-nos, the leaves, the frogs, the rhi-nos; If you keep read-ing, you'll learn a lot, 'bout things that o-thers won't tell you a-bout, if you ev-er want to find some-thing out, just read, read, read!

THE LIBRARY

Big books, little books,
Red books, blue books,
Picture books, pop-up books,
Books and books galore!

Fat books, skinny books,
Rhyming books, story books,
Animal books, music books
On the shelves and floor.

I must choose one right away.
It'll be awfully hard.
But once I'm ready, I will say,
"Here's my library card!"

MY COMPUTER

I have my ball. I have my bat.
I have my collection of bugs.
I have my rocks, my paint, my trike.
I have my share of hugs.

I also have a computer
To play games and learn online.
I never imagined having
A computer that's all mine.

I have a special user name
Set up just for me.
I need this name to log on.
It's my security.

As I sweep fingers across my screen,
It's wonderful to see
How quickly I can change things.
This is nothing like TV.

It helps me learn my letters
And count from one to ten,
Read my favorite stories
Like, *The Little Red Hen*.

Here I practice drawing
With colors of every hue,
And where I learn all the names
Of animals in the zoo.

I can visit countries,
Learn karate or kung foo.
If I want to call Grandma,
I can do that too!

I learn words to favorite songs,
Poems about snow and rain;
My computer allows me to listen
Over and over again.

Yes, I love my computer.
It helps me every day
Learn new things I need to know
In a totally different way!

I've Been Working On My Laptop
Tune: I've Been Working on the Railroad

American Folksong
Words by Boyer

I've been work-ing on my lap-top, all the live-long day. I've been work-ing on my lap-top, can't put this thing a - way. If some-one does not come stop me, I'll be here 'til morn. I sin-cere-ly love my lap-top. It's a lot of fun. Please come right a-way! I just want to say, my I. Q. lev-el's gone be-yond straight "A". Please come right a-way! I meas-ured it to-day; One thir-ty eight, hur-ray, hur-ray! I'm working with problems in cal-cu-lus, I can't e-ven add, and now I'm speak-ing Span-ish, "Ho-la", I'm ve-ry glad!

Dinosaurs!
Tune: Paw Paw Patch

American Folk Song
New Lyrics by Boyer

Verses

1. Stegosaurus, Spinasaurus, these are dinos;
Ankylosaurus, Tyrannasaurus, these are dinos;
Diplodocus, Velocirapter, these are dinos;
All their pictures are on my backpack!

2. Triceratops, Iquanodon, these are dinos;
Brachiosaurus, Apatosaurus, these are dinos;
Carnotaurus, Allosaurus, these are dinos;
They lived long ago and won't be back!

TRIANGLES, CIRCLES, AND SQUARES

Triangles, circles, and squares
Are shapes that I must know.
I see them all around me,
Up high and down below.

I love to make a circle
Along with all my friends.
It's where we sit for stories,
Listening from beginning to end.

A square is very simple.
It has four equal sides.
I see this shape wherever I go,
Indoors and outside.

The triangle is my favorite.
It has three points, you see.
Found on hats and sailboats
And in the symphony.

Shapes On Parade

Tune: Scotland's Burning

Traditional
New Lyrics by Boyer

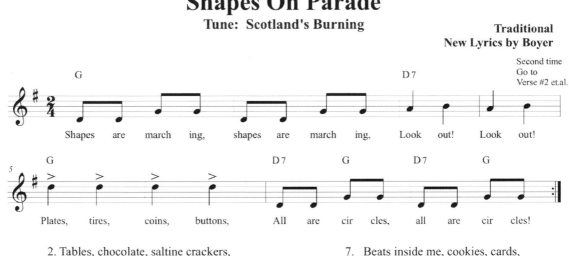

Shapes are marching, shapes are marching, Look out! Look out!

Plates, tires, coins, buttons, All are circles, all are circles!

2. Tables, chocolate, saltine crackers,
All are squares, all are squares!

3. Doors, TV's, smart phones, pillows,
Are rectangles, are rectangles!

4. Sailboat sails, slice of pizza,
Are triangles, are triangles!

5. Baseball home plate, buildings, okra,
Pentagons, pentagons!

6. Stop signs, big umbrellas,
Octagons, octagons!

7. Beats inside me, cookies, cards,
All are hearts, all are hearts!

8. Sky-high twinkles, sheriff's badges,
All are stars, all are stars!

9. Bolts, shapes on soccer balls,
Hexagons, hexagons!

10. Kites, tiles, shiny necklace,
All are diamonds, all are diamonds!

11. Eggs, mirrors, frames on photos,
All are ovals, all are ovals!

Counting Song

Mexican Folk Song

U - no, dos, y tres, cua - tro, cin - co seis,

sie - te, o - cho, nue - ve, I can count to diez.

La la la la la, la la la la la, la la la la la la;

La la la la la, la la la la la, la la la la la la.

Mein Hut

German Folk Song

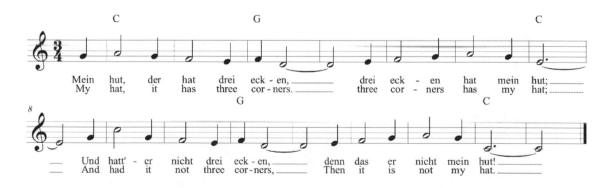

Mein hut, der hat drei eck - en,_____ drei eck - en hat mein hut;_____
My hat, it has three cor - ners._____ three cor - ners has my hat;_____

_____ Und hatt' - er nicht drei eck - en,_____ denn das er nicht mein hut!
_____ And had it not three cor - ners,_____ Then it is not my hat.

I CAN COUNT!

I can count. Oh yes I can!
I can count like a fireman.
One hose, two hoses, three hoses, four,
Five hoses, six hoses, seven hoses more.
Eight hoses, nine hoses, now there are ten.
Now let's count all over again.

I can count. Oh yes I can!
I can count like a policeman/policewoman.
One siren, two sirens, three sirens, four,
Five sirens, six sirens, seven sirens more.
Eight sirens, nine sirens, now there are ten.
Now let's count all over again.

I can count. Oh yes I can!
I can count like a baker.
One cake, two cakes, three cakes, four,
Five cakes, six cakes, seven cakes, more.
Eight cakes, nine cakes, now there are ten.
Now let's count all over again.

I can count. Oh yes I can!
I can count like a grocer.
One apple, two apples, three apples, four,
Five apples, six apples, seven apples more.

Eight apples, nine apples, now there are ten.
Now let's count all over again.

… I can count like a doctor.
One stitch, two stitches, etc.

… I can count like my teacher.
One problem, two problems, etc.

… I can count like a soldier.
One salute, two salutes, etc.

… I can count like a builder
One brick, two bricks, etc.

. . I can count like an athlete.
One sit-up, two sit-ups, etc.

. . I can count like a plumber.
One pipe, two pipes, etc.

. . I can count like a cashier,
One dollar, two dollars, etc.

Hickory Dickory Dock

Traditional

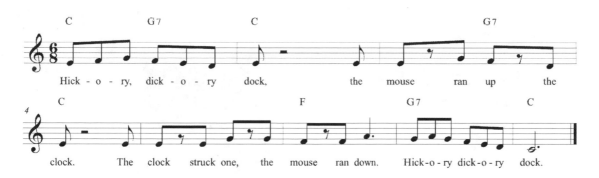

Hick - o - ry, dick - o - ry dock, the mouse ran up the clock. The clock struck one, the mouse ran down. Hick - o - ry dick - o - ry dock.

This Old Man

Traditional

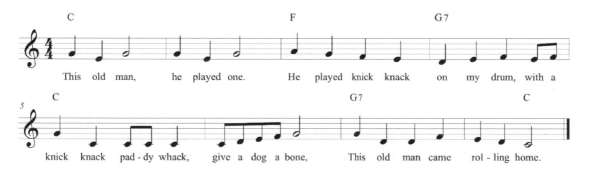

This old man, he played one. He played knick knack on my drum, with a knick knack pad - dy whack, give a dog a bone, This old man came rol - ling home.

1. This old man, he played two. . . .on my shoe.
2. This old man, he played three. . . .on my tree.
3. This old man, he played four. . .on my door.
4. This old man, he played five. .on my hive.
5. This old man, he played six. . .on my sticks.
6. This old man, he played seven. .up in Heaven.
7. This old man, he played eight. . .on my gate.
8. This old man, he played nine. . .on my line.
9. This old man, he played ten. on my chin.

BARNYARD SOUNDS

From dawn to dusk, I hear the sounds
Of the barnyard community;
Crowing and braying, quacking and neighing,
It's a wonderful place to be.

Cow's "moo" and the "cock-a-doodle doo"
Of Rooster's morning alarm
Begin the day in a startling way,
Waking us up on the farm.

Pig goes "oink" while Dog goes "woof."
Cat shadows a mouse.
Sheep goes "baa" and eats her hay
While Goat jumps on top of the house.

Horse goes neigh! It's a perfect day
To run and jump and play.
He invites Donkey to come along.
Rabbit has nothing to say.

Clucking of chickens and quacking of ducks
Add more to this symphony.
Reminds me of laughter, squeals, and yells
From children like you and me.

Old MacDonald

Traditional

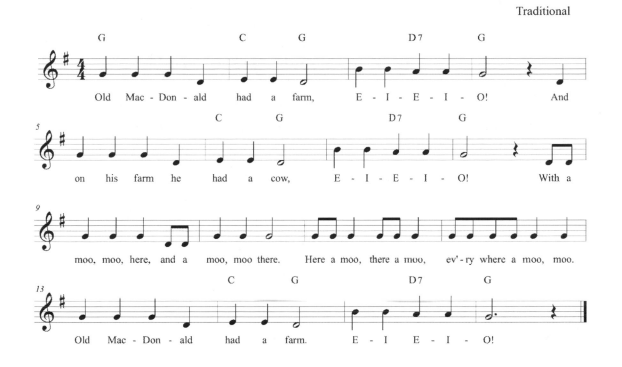

The Farmer in the Dell

Traditional

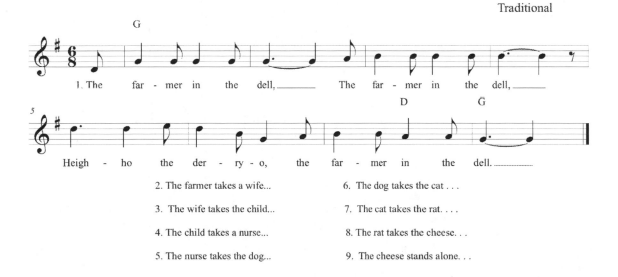

2. The farmer takes a wife...

3. The wife takes the child...

4. The child takes a nurse...

5. The nurse takes the dog...

6. The dog takes the cat...

7. The cat takes the rat....

8. The rat takes the cheese...

9. The cheese stands alone...

MY DAY AT THE ZOO

Where does one begin
A visit to the zoo?
With the apes and monkeys
Or the kangaroo?

One thing is for certain.
You'll need lots of time
To see the different animals
As they roam and climb.

Gorillas are most interesting.
They kinda act like us.
They love to eat bananas
And don't make lots of fuss.

Chimps are very different.
They spend their lives in trees,
Swinging back and forth on limbs
Like acrobats on a trapeze.

Lions are magnificent!
They beam with dignity.
Sitting on their haunches
For all the world to see.

The birdhouse offers children
A chance to see firsthand
Different kinds of birdies
That fly across our land.

Elephants are mighty!
And very smart, you know.
I love to see their long trunks
Swinging to and fro.

Giraffes are definite favorites.
Their long necks help them see
The leaves they love to eat for food
Found on the top of trees.

Penguins are most handsome
In suits of black and white.
They love to dive in water,
Which is often cold as ice.

Zebras look like horses,
Striped in brown and white.
They move in herds across the plains.
They are a glorious sight!

Sea lions are a favorite
In almost every zoo.
They swim and clap for everyone.
They know just what to do.

Suddenly, I'm awfully tired.
I cannot carry on.
I need some popcorn and some juice,
And then I want to go home.

One Elephant

Traditional

One el-e-phant went out to play, out on a spi-der's___ web one day.

He had such e-nor-mous fun, he called for a-noth-er el-e-phant to come.

2. Two elephants went out to play . . .
3. Three elephants went out to play . . .
4. Four elephants went out to play . . .
5. Five elephants wents out to play . . .

Los Elefantes

Spanish Children's Counting Song

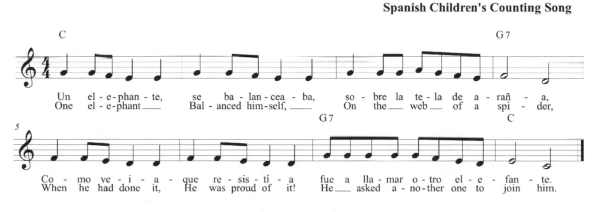

Un el-e-phan-te, se ba-lan-cea-ba, so-bre la te-la de a-rañ- a,
One el-e-phant___ Bal-anced him-self,___ On the___ web___ of a spi- der,

Co - mo ve-i- a - que re-sis-tí- a fue a lla-mar o-tro el-e- fan- te.
When he had done it, He was proud of it! He___ asked a-no-ther one to join him.

2. Dos elefantes . . . 3. Tres elephantes. . . 4. Cuatro elefantes. . . 5. Cinco elefantes. . .

Liang Zhi Lao Hu
Two Tigers
Tune: Are You Sleeping

Taiwanese Folk Tune

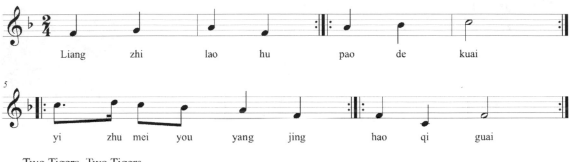

Liang   zhi   lao   hu   pao   de   kuai

yi   zhu   mei   you   yang   jing   hao   qi   guai

Two Tigers, Two Tigers
Run so fast, run so fast
One has no ears,
One has no tail,
So strange! So strange!

THE OCEAN

Take me to the ocean!
Take me to the sea!
There is not another place
That I'd rather be.

Covered with lots of sunscreen,
I am able to see
That this stuff keeps sunrays
From really hurting me.

On the beach, I start my day
Collecting shells and things
That lay like gemstones in the sand,
A gift the tide oft brings.

Building a sandcastle is a must!
That's what people do.
With my pail and shovel,
I can do it too.

When my castle's finished,
I want to understand
Why sea turtles lay their eggs
In the ocean's sand.

I run and play a little more.
Then, dressed with water wings,
I'm carefully carried to the sea
While arms around me cling.

I feel the ocean water.
I taste the salty sea.
I look around and figure out
I'm as tiny as a flea.

As I am carried to the shore,
I can honestly say
That I have had a lot of fun
At the beach today.

Let's Go to the Ocean
Tune: Paw Paw Patch

American Singing Game

Come on ___ guys, let's go to the o - cean. Come on ___ guys, let's go to the o - cean.

Come on ___ guys, let's go to the o - cean. Get your gear and don't for - get a snack.

2. Sharks and dolphins, all in the ocean.
Sharks and dolphins, all in the ocean,
Sharks and dolphins, all in the ocean,
Playing and a riding on the great humpback.

3. Octopus and jellyfish, all in the ocean,
Octopus and jellyfish, all in the ocean.
Octopus and jellyfish, all in the ocean,
Playing and a riding on the great humpback.

4. Stingrays, starfish, all in the ocean.. .

5. Oysters and clams, all in the ocean.. . .

6. Crabs and lobsters, all in the ocean.. . .

7. Eels and puffer fish all in the ocean.. . .

8. Swordfish, flying fish, all in the ocean. . .

9. Pacific, Atlantic are names of the oceans,
Artic, Indian, are names of the oceans,
Then there's the southern one, called Antarctic
There's sea-life in every one.

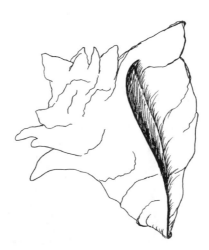

Down By the Bay

American Nonsense Song

2. "Did you ever see a whale, with a polka dot tail?"
3. "Did you ever see a fly wearing a tie?"
4. "Did you ever see a bear, combing his hair?"
5. "Did you ever see llamas, eating their pajamas?"
6. "Did you ever see a flea, babysitting me?"
6. "Did you ever have a time when you couldn't make a rhyme?"

A Visit to the Ocean

Tune: My Bonnie Lies Over the Ocean

Folk Song
New Lyrics by Boyer

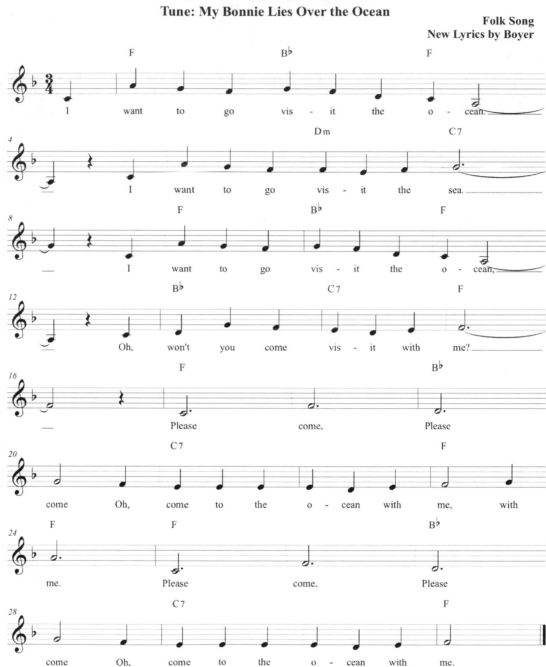

Let's Dance

Words and Music by Rene Boyer

Let's dance the sam - ba. Let's dance me - rang - ue.

Let's dance the sal - sa, Now we'll all get down and cha-cha too.

The Fishy
Tune: Shortnin' Bread

African American Folk Song

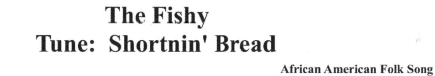

1. Let's go see my fish - y, fish - y, fish - y, Let's go see my fish - y, swim a - round.
2. Let's go see my fish - y, fish - y, fish - y, Let's go see my fish swim up and down.

THE AQUARIUM

The Aquarium is a special place
For everyone to see
Marine life that's abundant.
Under three, you get in free.

I always head first to the sharks.
I want to see them swim
Deep below the surface
Where light is very dim.

Sharks come in many sizes.
They smell most everything.
With teeth that drop out, then grow back,
They're very interesting!

Stingrays glide like spaceships.
They move so fast and free,
Twisting, turning as they go
Across the deep blue sea.

When they tire, you'll find them
Hiding beneath the sand.
With eyes up top and mouths below,
They'll sting you if they can.

Eels are slender, ribbon-like fish
That slither to and fro.
They live in shallow water.
That's where they like to go.

When you see them late at night,
They look just like a tree,
Lit up with cool colors
Of yellow, blue, and green.

The puffer fish looks very odd.
It puffs up then forms spikes
That poison any other fish
Who try to take a bite.

Tropical fish are amazing!
They come in every hue.
Green, red, purple, orange,
Yellow, black, and blue.

Some have dots, and others stripes.
Some have fluffy manes.
Some look simply elegant,
While some of them are plain.

Turtles are great swimmers!
By alternating arms and feet,
They really show us how to swim;
Watching them is neat!

Sea stars are most popular
Because of their five arms.
Striking colors and hardened skin
Protect sea stars from harm.

Dolphins are athletic.
They love to jump and leap
In sync with one another,
Into the ocean deep.

They often hunt together,
Surrounding chosen prey.
When they have enough to eat,
They will go and play.

Dolphins have a unique tail.
It's like our fingerprint.
No two dolphins are the same.
You can count on it.

Jellyfish will sting you
If you're in the sea.
Inside the aquarium,
You're as safe as safe can be.

They look so very delicate,
Like a parachute
Sewn together with translucent silk
That you can see right through.

Alligators are a must
Of marine life kids should see
Because they are so powerful
And fast as fast can be.

With jagged teeth inside their mouths,
They'll run fast either way,
Out of water or into it;
They always get their prey.

Called the rain forest of the sea,
A coral reef is home
To the tiniest marine animals
That don't like being alone.

A coral is an animal
That lives inside its shell.
A reef is the community
In which they safely dwell.

Other creatures make their homes
In the coral reef,
Where they live from day to day
In merciful relief!

The aquarium is truly a wonderful place,
And it is my greatest wish
That we go often to look and learn
About our marine life and fish.

Five Little Speckled Frogs

Traditional

1. Five lit - tle speck-led frogs, sat on a speck-led log, eat - ing some
2. One jumped in - to the pool, where it was nice and cool, now there are

most de - li - cious bugs; Yum, yum.
just four speck - led

frogs. Croak! Croak!

2. Four little speckled frogs.. .   4. Two little speckled frogs . .
3. Three little speckled frogs. .   5. One little speckled frogs. . .

6.. . No more, no speckled frogs. . .
Sitting on a speckled log,
Croak! Croak!

Kaeru No Uta Ga
The Frog's Song

Japanese Folk Song

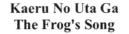

Ka - e - ru no u - ta - ga. Ki - ko - e - te, ku - ru - yo.
Lis - ten to the frog - gies song. We can hear it, all day long.

Gwa, gwa, gwa, gwa! Ge - ro, ge - ro, ge - ro, ge - ro, Gwa, gwa, gwa!
Ribbit, ribbit, ribbit, ribbit! Rib - bit, rib - bit, rib - bit, rib - bit, Croak, croak, croak!

MY STAR, MY MOON, MY SUN

I love the twinkling stars at night.
I love the big, round moon.
I love the sun that lights my day.
It looks like a yellow balloon.

I feel they are a part of me—
My stars, my moon, my sun.
They smile their shining light on me.
They shine for everyone.

Starlight

American Folk Song

Star light, star - bright, first star I see to - night.

Wish I may, wish I might, have the wish I wish to - night.

Twinkle Twinkle Little Star

Traditional

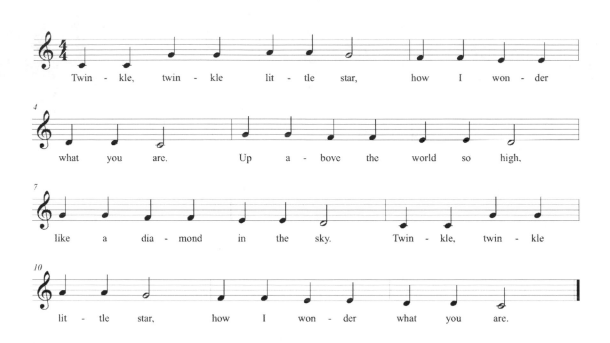

Aiken Drum

Scottish Folk Song

64

My Trip Through the Solar System
Tune: Here We Go Looby Loo

Traditional
Words by Rene Boyer

Here we go round the moon. Here we go round the sun.

Here we go round the moon, Oh, what a day of great fun!

2. I see the twink-ling stars. I see the plan-et Mars. I see the

plan-et of Ju-pi-ter, Oh my, it is quite large!

Additional Verses:

3. I see all Saturn's rings.
Uranus looks blue-green.
Neptune's planet has so much gas,
The most I've ever seen.

4. Pluto is far away.
It looks so dull and gray.
You need a powerful telescope,
To see this planet today.

5. It's time to head back home.
Towards Mercury, here I come.
I must be very careful of you,
You're too close to the sun.

6. There's Venus up ahead.
I know it's hot, "Oh dread!"
It's shining brighteer than all the rest,
I feel it on my head.

7. I've come back down to Earth.
The planet of my birth,
The other ones were so much fun,
But Earth, to me, is first.

Oh, Mister Sun

Children's Song

Oh, Mis - ter Sun, Sun, Mis - ter gold - en sun, won't you please shine down on me. Oh, Mis - ter Sun, Sun, Mis - ter gold-en sun, hi - ding be - hind that tree. There are lit - tle child - ren who are ask - ing you, to please come out so we can play with you, Oh, Mis - ter Sun, Sun, Mis - ter gold-en sun, Won't you please shine down on me.

2. Oh, Mr. Moon, Moon, bright and silvery moon,
Please shine down on me.
Oh, Mr. Moon, Moon, bright and silvery moon,
Hiding behind that tree.
While the sun is sleeping and the stars are bright
You're the one who will provide my light.
Oh, Mr. Moon, Moon, bright and silvery moon,
Please shine down on me.

3. Oh, little stars, stars, little twinkling stars,
Please shine down on me.
Oh, little stars, stars, little twinkling stars,
Shine bright so I can see,
I've a special wish that I will wish tonight,
So show your colors, red and blue and white,
Oh little stars, stars, twinkling little stars,
Please shine down on me.

IT'S RAINING

Hurray! Hurray! It's raining.
It's time for my little raincoat.
I mustn't forget my brand-new boots
And of course my special umbrella!

I wish to splash in puddles,
Get wet from head to toe.
My, oh my! What a special day.
Hurry, I'm ready to go!

What's the Weather?
Tune: Clementine

Traditional

What's the wea-ther? What's the wea-ther? What's the wea-ther like to-day? What's the wea-ther? What's the wea-ther? I must go out-side to play? Is it cloud-y? Is it sun-ny? Will it rain or will it snow? What's the wea-ther? What's the wea-ther? What's the wea-ther? Do you know?

It's Raining, It's Pouring

Traditional

It's rain - ing. It's pour - ing. The old man is snor - ing. He went to bed and bumped his head, and didn't wake up 'til morn - ing.

My Rainbow
Tune: Bluebird

Boyer

Red and o - range, in my rain - bow, Yel - low, green, in my rain - bow,
Sev - en col - ors, in my rain - bow, Sev - en col - ors, in my rain - bow,

Blue and in - di - go, in my rain - bow; Vi - o - let is in my rain - bow too.
Sev - en col - ors are in my rain - bow; Lots of pret - ty col - ors for me and too.

Let's Take a Walk

Boyer

Let's take a walk through the flowers to - day, through the flowers to - day, through the flowers to - day.

Let's take a walk through the flowers to - day to see what we can see.

Take an imaginary walk through the flowers to see roses, sunflowers, daffodils, daisies etc.
Take an imaginary walk to the farm, the zoo, the beach, the park, the city, etc.

My Garden

I have a little garden.
It's where I like to be,
With flowers in the springtime
Looking up at me.

I love the hardy pansies.
I love the crocus too.
They always bloom in early spring
In colors of every hue.

Daffodils are glorious.
You see them everywhere.
Blankets of yellow cover lawns,
Swaying gently in the air!

Tulips seem to shoot straight up
On light green colored stems.
With blooms of yellow, red, and pink,
They look like delicate gems.

Lilacs, along with hyacinths,
Fill the fresh spring air.
With perfumed scents and colors,
Nothing can compare.

My allium plant is interesting,
Shaped just like a ball.
It's delicate and fluffy
And different from them all.

Oh, what beautiful flowers,
In all their majesty,
Growing in my garden.
I think they all love me.

I Had A Little Nut Tree

Folk Song

I had a lit - tle nut tree, noth - ing would it bear,
But a sil - ver nut - meg, and a gold - en pear. The King of Spain's daugh - ter
came to vis - it me. and all for the sake of my lit - tle nut tree.

BUTTERFLY

How beautiful its color!
How delicately it flies.
I would like to speak to it
When it passes by.

I'd love to follow it in my yard
To see what it can see.
I wonder as I look at it,
Is it looking back at me?

Pretty Pretty Butterfly
Tune: Twinkle Twinkle Little Star

Traditional
New Lyrics by Boyer

Pret - ty pret - ty but - ter - fly. I can see you but - ter - fly. Float-ing on the gen - tle breeze,
Wings that flut - ter, wings that fly, I can see you but - ter - fly. Float-ting on the gen - tle breeze,

Land-ing on the flowers and trees. Pret - ty pret - ty but - ter - fly, You are wel - come, please stop by.
Land-ing on the flowers and trees. Wings that flut - ter, wings that fly, Good bye, good bye, but - ter - fly.

FROGGIE

I need a box. I need some grass.
I need my little boots.
I need some dirt, some worms and bugs,
Perhaps a little fruit.

I really hope to find him
Living near the creek
Where he hops from stone to stone.
I saw him there last week.

At first he was a tadpole,
Swimming near a log.
Something happened to him.
Now he is a frog.

I want to ask him if he'd come
Visit me for a day.
I'll introduce him to my friends,
And then we can all play.

I'll take him back at day's end
So he can fall asleep
Sitting on his lily pad,
Where the water is not so deep.

Kerplunck Went the Little Green Frog

Traditional

Ker - plunck, went the lit - tle green frog one day, Ker - plunck, went the lit - tle green frog. Ker -

plunck, went the lit - tle green frog one day, Ker - plunck, Ker - plunck, Ker - plunck!

EIGHT LEGS

Eight legs climbing to the top.
Eight legs climbing down,
Weaving threads of sticky silk
Without a single sound.

The Eensy Weensy Spider

Children's Song

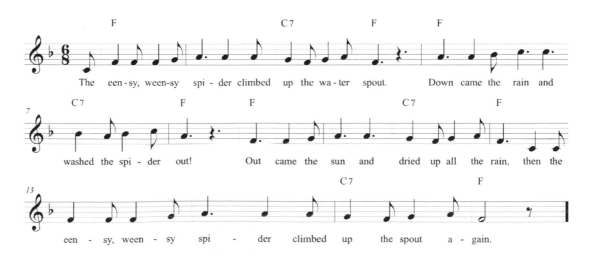

The een - sy, ween - sy spi - der climbed up the wa - ter spout. Down came the rain and

washed the spi - der out! Out came the sun and dried up all the rain, then the

een - sy, ween - sy spi - der climbed up the spout a - gain.

THE LADYBUG

She has a little red body.
She has six little legs.
She has black spots on top of her wings
And antennae on top of her head.

She loves to eat the aphids
Off plants in my garden green,
Then fly around so all can see
The beauty that summer brings!

Ladybug
Tune: Jingle Bell

James Lord Pierpont
New Lyrics by Boyer

Lady bug, Lady bug, you have work to - day.

When the a - phids all are gone, will you come and play?

La - dy bug, La - dy bug, you're like a fan - cy dot.

Paint - ed in your black and red, I like you a lot.

ANTS

There are hundreds of them!
Thousands of them!
Marching everywhere!
Building sandy houses
In the summer air.

My magnifying glass is ready
So I see crystal clear
Exactly what they're doing.
They do not know I'm here.

I see them carry green leaves
And tiny blades of grass.
They are very busy
As one by one they pass.

Is this what their life is about?
Working every day?
Perhaps I should be busy too,
But I prefer to play!

The Ants Are A-Coming
Tune: The Campbells Are Coming

Scottish Folk Song
c. 1745
Adapted Tune by Boyer

1. The ants are a-com-ing, hur-rah, hur-rah! The ants are a com-ing, hur-rah, hur-rah! The
2. They're build-ing their hous-es, hur-rah, hur-rah! They're build-ing their hous-es, hur-rah, hur-rah! They're
3. They're tun-nel-ing un-der, hur-rah, hur-rah! They're tun-nel-ing un-der, hur-rah, hur-rah! They're

ants are a-com-ing, hur-rah, hur-rah! They're com-ing in hun-dreds, hur-rah, hur-rah!
build-ing their hous-es, hur-rah, hur-rah! They're build-ing their hous-es of wood and straw.
tun-nel-ing un-der, hur-rah! hur-rah! These ants are so awe-some like Ma and Pa!

A Visit to the Veggie Farm

The veggie farm's spectacular!
A wondrous place to see.
Rows and rows of veggies grow,
Loaded with vitamin C.

With sun and soil and daily rain
And someone to hoe weeds,
Veggies sprout from tiny seeds
To fill an important need.

They color fields in red and yellow,
Purple, orange, and brown,
But nothing compares to leafy greens
That sprout up all around.

Corn, eggplant, lettuce,
Cabbage, okra, kale.
Onions, peas, and carrots
Grow by peck and bale.

Potatoes and tomatoes,
Spinach, squash, and beans.
Beets, cucumber, and broccoli
And good ol' turnip greens.

These are some examples
Of veggies that help me grow
And keep my body healthy
From my head down to my toe.

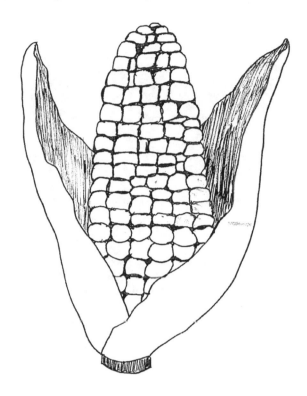

Oats, Peas, Beans and Barley Grow

Folk Song

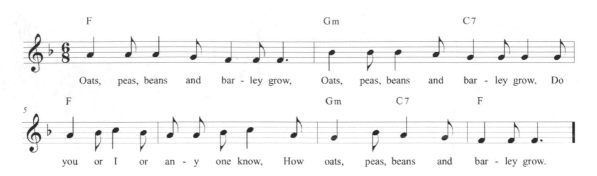

Oats, peas, beans and bar - ley grow, Oats, peas, beans and bar - ley grow, Do you or I or an - y one know, How oats, peas, beans and bar - ley grow.

2. First the farmer sows his seeds.
Stands erect and takes his ease,
He stamps his foot and claps his hands,
And turns around to view his lands.

3. Next the farmer waters the seeds,
Stands erect and takes his ease,
He stamps his foot and claps his hands,
And turns around to view his lands.

4. Next the farmer hoes the weeds,
Stands erect and takes his ease,
He stamps his foot and claps his hands,
And turns around to view his lands.

5. Last the farmer harvests his seeds,
Stands erect and takes his ease,
He stamps his foot and claps his hands,
And turns around to view his land.

John the Rabbit

African American Folk Song

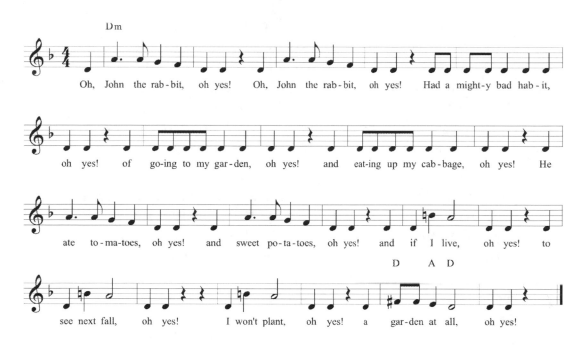

Oh, John the rab-bit, oh yes! Oh, John the rab-bit, oh yes! Had a might-y bad hab-it,

oh yes! of go-ing to my gar-den, oh yes! and eat-ing up my cab-bage, oh yes! He

ate to-ma-toes, oh yes! and sweet po-ta-toes, oh yes! and if I live, oh yes! to

see next fall, oh yes! I won't plant, oh yes! a gar-den at all, oh yes!

SUMMER CAMP

When the month of June rolls 'round,
There's something I must do—
Ready myself for summer camp
To hang with friends and crew.

My water bottle and swimwear
Are in an old backpack,
Along with towel and goggles,
A lunch and special snack.

I know I can't wear dress shoes
Or sandals with toes out.
I need my trusty rubber soles
To climb and run about.

Every morning, we gather
To sing our special song.
All the campers join in
With voices loud and strong.

Arts and crafts are fun.
We do them every day.
We paint, paste, cut, and draw
In our own creative way.

Everyone goes swimming
In a natural lake
We also learn to paddle boats.
It's a piece of cake.

Sometimes we gather in evenings
Around a huge campfire.
We eat and listen to guitars
And relax in the cool night air.

Yes, I'm ready to go to camp,
Where I'll spend each day
Exploring the world around me
In a most enjoyable way.

Make New Friends

Traditional

Make new friends, but keep the old. One is sil-ver and the o-ther gold.

Alabama Gal

American Folk Song

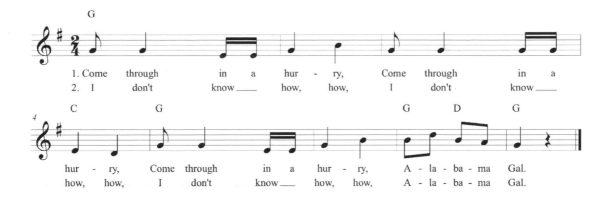

1. Come through in a hur – ry, Come through in a
2. I don't know ___ how, how, I don't know ___

hur – ry, Come through in a hur – ry, A – la – ba – ma Gal.
how, how, I don't know ___ how, how, A – la – ba – ma Gal.

A Ram Sam Sam

Moroccan Children's Song

(Alternate fisted hands to the beat.)

(Shake both hands in the air.)

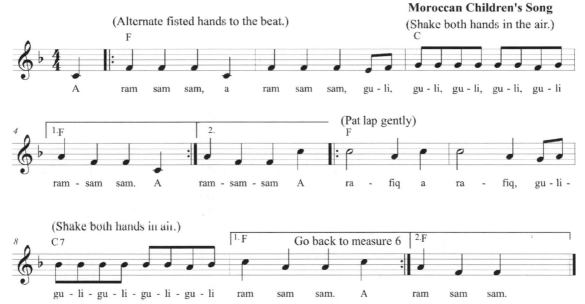

A ram sam sam, a ram sam sam, gu – li, gu – li, gu – li, gu – li, gu – li

(Pat lap gently)

ram – sam sam. A ram – sam – sam A ra – fiq a ra – fiq, gu – li –

(Shake both hands in air.)

Go back to measure 6

gu – li – gu – li – gu – li – gu – li ram sam sam. A ram sam sam.

Che Che Koolay

Folk Song from Ghana

Leader: Che che koo - lay, Children Che che koo - lay, Leader Che che ko - fee - sa, Children Che che ko - fee - sa,

Ko-fee sa-lan - ga, Ko-fee sa-lan - ga, Ka-ka - shee lan - ga, Ka-ka - shee-lan - ga,

Whoops, ah lay lay, Whoops, ah lay, lay, Whoops, ah lay, lay, Hey!

Funga Alafia

Funga Alafia is from Western Africa.
It is in the Yoruba language.
It means welcome and blessings.

African Welcome Song

Fun-ga a - la - fia, Ah-shay, Ah-shay. Fun-ga a - la - fia, Ah-shay, Ah-shay.

Ah-shay, Ah-shay. Ah-shay, Ah-shay Ah-shay, Ah-shay, Ah-shay, Ah-shay.

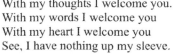

With my thoughts I welcome you.
With my words I welcome you
With my heart I welcome you
See, I have nothing up my sleeve.

MY SPECIAL FRIEND

My special friend was waiting
When I arrived at home.
She sat and watched me every day.
She never left me alone.

She watched me learn to roll and sit
She watched me learn to crawl.
She watched me pull up, then to walk,
Toddling down the hall.

She never ever fussed at me,
No matter what I did.
Though I was often a stinker,
She knew I was just a kid.

She'll always be my special friend.
This I really know,
Because she follows me around
Wherever I choose to go.

Bingo

Traditional

There was a far-mer had a dog, and Bin-go was his name-o.
B - I - N - G - O! B - I - N - G - O B - I -
N - G - O and Bin-go was his name-o!

Kaeru No Uta Ga
The Frog's Song

Japanese Folk Song

Ka - e - ru   no   u - ta - ga.   Ki - ko - e - te,   ku - ru - yo
Lis - ten   to   the   frog - gies   song.   We   can   hear   it,   All   day   long.

Gwa!   Gwa!   Gwa!   Gwa!   Ge - ro, Ge - ro, Ge - ro, Ge - ro,   Gwa! Gwa! Gwa!
Ribbit!   Ribbit!   Ribbit!   Ribbit!   Rib-bit, Rib-bit, Rib-bit, Rib-bit,   Croak, Croak, Croak!

MY VISIT TO THE DOCTOR'S OFFICE

The doctor's office is the place
They take me right away
When my nose is running
And I'm coughing night and day.

Sometimes I have a temperature.
I feel so frail and weak.
I don't feel much like playing.
I simply want to sleep.

If I have an earache,
I know that something's wrong.
I need to see a doctor.
I feel it in my bones.

The doctor uses a stethoscope
To examine me.
The diagnosis that she gives,
"You need vitamin D."

Although I've shed my share of tears,
I'm happy to always see
A nurse with a great big lollipop,
Waiting just for me.

Miss Lucy Had A Baby

Playground Chant

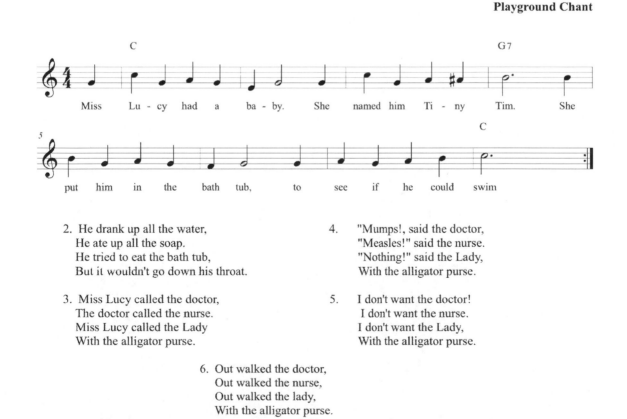

Miss Lu - cy had a ba - by. She named him Ti - ny Tim. She
put him in the bath tub, to see if he could swim

2. He drank up all the water,
   He ate up all the soap.
   He tried to eat the bath tub,
   But it wouldn't go down his throat.

3. Miss Lucy called the doctor,
   The doctor called the nurse.
   Miss Lucy called the Lady
   With the alligator purse.

4. "Mumps!", said the doctor,
   "Measles!" said the nurse.
   "Nothing!" said the Lady,
   With the alligator purse.

5. I don't want the doctor!
   I don't want the nurse.
   I don't want the Lady,
   With the alligator purse.

6. Out walked the doctor,
   Out walked the nurse,
   Out walked the lady,
   With the alligator purse.

Five Little Monkeys

Traditional

2. Four little monkeys jumping on the bed,
One fell off and bumped his head.
The mama called the doctor and the doctor said,
"No more monkeys jumping on the bed."

3. Three little monkeys. . .

4. Two little monkeys. . .

5. One little monkey jumping on the bed,
He fell off and bumped his head.
The mama called the doctor and the doctor said,
"There are no more monkeys to jump on the bed."

John Brown's Baby

Folk Song

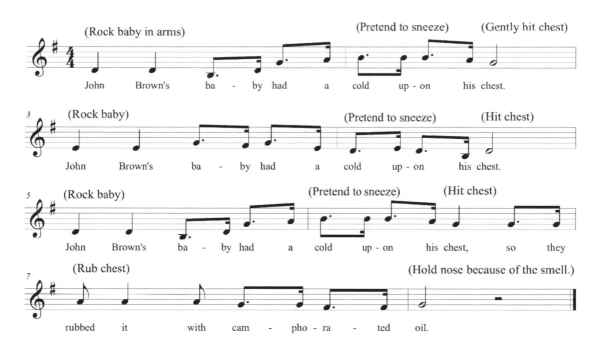

(Rock baby in arms)   (Pretend to sneeze)   (Gently hit chest)

John Brown's ba - by had a cold up - on his chest.

(Rock baby)   (Pretend to sneeze)   (Hit chest)

John Brown's ba - by had a cold up - on his chest.

(Rock baby)   (Pretend to sneeze)   (Hit chest)

John Brown's ba - by had a cold up - on his chest, so they

(Rub chest)   (Hold nose because of the smell.)

rubbed it with cam - pho - ra - ted oil.

THE DENTIST

"Your little teeth are gleaming,"
My dentist told me today.
"Whatever you are doing,
Keep it up the very same way."

I said, "I brush them in the morning
And then again at night."
I said, "I love to brush my teeth.
I call them my pearly whites!"

I was given a brand-new toothbrush
And showed a special way
To clean both top and bottom
To avoid future tooth decay.

I felt so very proud of me
As I turned to say good-bye.
Then smiled up at the dentist and said,
"I'll see you in July."

Brush, Brush, Brush Your Teeth
Tune: Row, Row, Row Your Boat

Traditional
New Lyrics by Boyer

Brush, brush, brush your teeth, each and ev'ry day.
This will help your pearl - y whites, have no tooth de-cay!

MY LOOSE TOOTH

I had a loose tooth a while ago.
It wiggled, and it jiggled, and it moved just so.
Until one morning, it just fell out.
I couldn't help it. I started to shout!

I looked into the mirror and started to moan.
I could not believe my tooth was gone!
I called Mommy and Daddy to see
What on earth had happened to me.

I told them, "My tooth fell out!"
They gave me hugs and turned me about.
They looked at me and said, "Don't cry.
That little tooth had to go bye-bye."

It's important for you to know,
Another tooth will follow in a month or so.
One that is stronger and will always help you
With whichever foods you wish to chew

FALLING LEAVES

Leaves are gently falling.
They're drifting all around.
Yellow, red, orange, and brown,
They're falling to the ground.

Their colors are so beautiful!
I don't have words to say.
But one thing I would like to **know,**
"What makes them change this **way?**"

A month ago, they all were green,
Glistening after the rain.
Breezes gently swept them,
Creating a melodious strain.

But now those days grow shorter,
And summertime is gone.
Something magical has happened.
Something's come undone.

It's sad to see them leave this way.
But oh, what a glorious sight
To see their majesty of color
As they appear in the autumn light.

I really think that they all know
That winter will soon appear
And that it's time for them to go
And start again next year.

Autumn Leaves
Tune: London Bridge

Traditional

Au - tumn leaves are fall - ing down, fall - ing down, fall - ing down.

Au - tumn leaves are fall - ing down, fall - ing to the ground.

2. See their colors red and brown, red and brown, red and brown,
See their colors red and brown, all around the town.

3. I see yellow, orange too, orange too, orange too,
I see yellow, orange too, lots for me and you.

4. Pick some up and throw them high, throw them high, throw them high,
Pick some up and throw them high, try to reach the sky.

APPLE-PICKING TIME IS HERE!

Apple-picking time is here!
It happens in the fall each year
When apple trees have fruit to bear
Shall I pick one? Do I dare?

McIntosh and Granny Smith,
Fuji, Pippin, Honeycrisp,
Red Delicious, Jonagold,
All great apples, so I'm told.

I need help from someone tall.
I can't reach. I'm much too small.
Who will lift me in the air?
I want that one, way up there.

Steady now, I'm ready to pluck.
Oops! I dropped it—just my luck!
One more boost please. I'll get one.
Then I'll eat it. Yum! Yum! Yum!

It's Apple Pickin' Time
Tune: The Farmer in the Dell

Traditional
New Lyrics by Boyer

It's ap - ple pick - in' time! It's ap - ple pick - in' time! Ev' - ry - bo - dy come a - long, It's ap - ple pick - in' time!

2. They're on the apple tree.
They're on the apple tree.
Run, Run, Let's have some fun.
They're on the apple tree.

3. Let's pick one off the tree.
Let's pick one off the tree.
That one's high and that's one's low,
Let's pick one off the tree.

4. We all should take a bite.
We all should take a bite.
Even if you're missing teeth,
We all should take a bite.

5. The juice is streaming down.
The juice is streaming down.
We're sticky and we're all a mess,
The juice is streaming down.

6. It's time to bake some pies,
It's time to bake some pies,
Applesauce and fritters too,
It's time to bake some pies.

Farmer Brown Had Five Red Apples

Children's Finger Play

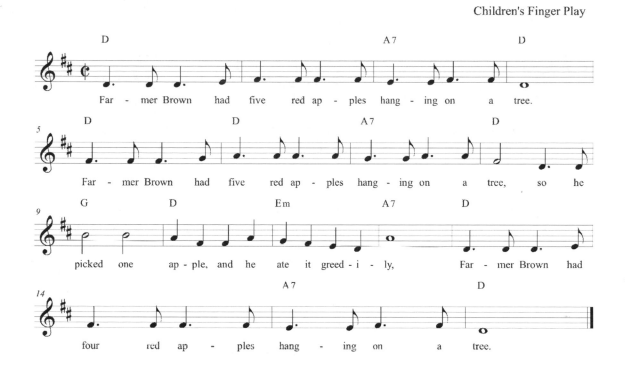

Far - mer Brown had five red ap - ples hang - ing on a tree.
Far - mer Brown had five red ap - ples hang - ing on a tree, so he
picked one ap - ple, and he ate it greed - i - ly, Far - mer Brown had
four red ap - ples hang - ing on a tree.

Hop Old Squirrel

American Folk Song

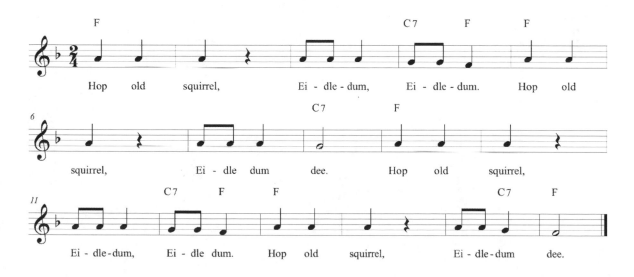

Hop old squirrel, Ei - dle - dum, Ei - dle - dum. Hop old
squirrel, Ei - dle dum dee. Hop old squirrel,
Ei - dle - dum, Ei - dle dum. Hop old squirrel, Ei - dle - dum dee.

The Earth Is Our Mother

Traditional Hopi Indian Chant

The earth is our mo - ther, we must take care of her, The earth is our mo - ther We must take care of her. Hey yan - na, Ho yan - na Hey yan yan. Hey yan - na, Ho yan - na Hey yan yan.

Hep-A, Hep-A Nay
A Blessing For Our Earth

Traditional Native American Chant

Hep-a, hep-a, nay nay. Hep-a, hep-a, nay nay. Hep-a, hep-a, nay nay. Hep-a, hep-a, nay nay. Hep-a nay, yan-na hen-nay, yo way! (Clap, clap) Hep-a-nay, yan-na hen-nay, yo way! (Clap, clap)

MY BIRTHDAY PARTY

My birthday party is really fun.
My friends are everywhere.
Bringing presents with ribbons and bows.
It's really quite an affair!

Balloons and streamers accent walls;
Also the tables and chairs
Are covered with lots of little toys,
Lions, giraffes, and bears.

Everyone wears a birthday hat,
And all are ready to play
Lots of games and activities
Designed for my special day.

Pizza, pretzels, carrots. and chips,
Along with puffed corn balls
Are served on colorful birthday plates,
Ready to be eaten by all.

The cake is an artistic masterpiece,
Prepared just for me.
My favorite of course is chocolate,
But I'll have to wait and see.

When I blow out my candles
And eat my birthday cake,
I know that by tomorrow
I'll have a tummy ache.

It's My Birthday!
Tune: Do You Know the Muffin Man

Traditional
New Lyrics by Boyer

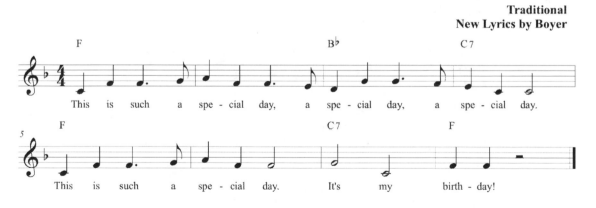

When Billy Was One

Folk Song

1. When Bil - ly was one,   he liked to suck his
2. When Bil - ly was two,   he learned to tie his

thumb;   One, Bil-ly Bil - ly,   one Bil-ly Bil - ly,   half - past one.
shoe,   Two Bil-ly Bil - ly,   two Bil-ly Bil - ly,   half - past two.

3. When Biily was three, he learned to climb a tree. . .
4. When Billy was four, he learned to unlock doors. . .
5. When Billy was five, he learned to swim and dive. .
6. When Billy was six, he learned to build with sticks. . .
7. When Billy was seven, he knew the planets in Heaven. .
8. When Billy was eight, he learned to roller skate. . .
9. When Billy was nine, he ordered games online. . .
10. When Billy was ten, he lost his ballpoint pen. . .
11. When Billy was eleven, he caught his bus at seven. . .
12. When Billy was twelve, He organized his shelves. . . .

Twelve Months of the Year
Tune: John Brown Had A Little Indian

Lyrics by Boyer

1. Jan - u - ar - y, Feb-ru - ar - y,   March and A - pril,   May and June, Ju - ly and Au - gust Sep-

tem - ber, Oct - o - ber, No - vem - ber, De-cem - ber,   these   are the twelve months   of the year.

2. Everybody here, has a birthday!
Everybody here, has a birthday!
Everybody here, has a birthday!
It is the best day of the year.

3. April 2nd is my birthday,
April 2nd is my birthday,
April 2nd is my birthday,
It is the best day of the year.

HOLIDAYS

Every year I celebrate
Special holidays,
Days I know will still be 'round
When I'm old and gray.

On New Year's Day I always think
About my contribution
To self, to school, and family.
I call this, "my resolution."

There are famous people
Everyone should know.
Martin Luther King was one of them
Who helped our nation grow.

Our present and past presidents
Are given a special day
So we can stop to honor them
In a fun yet thoughtful way.

Because I like my friends at school,
I must remember them all
By giving each a valentine.
I buy them at the mall.

St Patrick's Day permits me,
During the early spring,
To say good-bye to winter.
That's why I dress in green.

In springtime I am ready
To hunt for colorful eggs,
Hidden by a fluffy bunny
With two ears atop his head.

Mother's Day is important,
Because my mom must know
How much I truly treasure her
And that I love her so.

Memorial, Labor, and Veteran's Day
Honor many in our land.
Skies are lit with fireworks
With a parade and marching band.

Father's Day happens every June
And directly relates to me,
'Cause if it were not for my dad,
I wouldn't be here, you see.

July Fourth has fireworks too.
It's the birthday of the USA.
Picnics, grilling, water sports,
Fun, fun, fun all day!

Thanksgiving is for family.
Everyone gathers to eat
Lots and lots of special foods,
Including delicious treats.

During the month of December,
Most little girls and boys
Are given very special gifts.
My favorites, of course, are toys.

All in all, I'm happy
Whenever there's a holiday.
It's a time to spend with family
And a great time for me to play.

Martin Luther King

Tune: Somebody's Knocking At My Door

Lyrics by Rene Boyer

Oh, When the Saints

Words by Katherine E. Purvis
Music by James M. Black

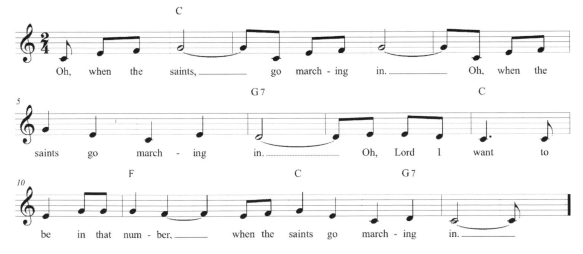

Love Somebody

Traditional

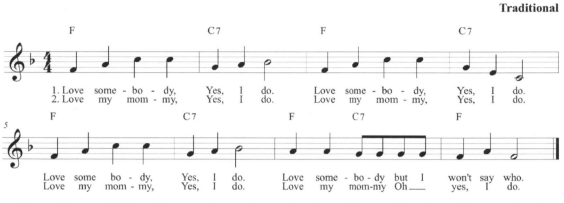

1. Love some - bo - dy, Yes, I do. Love some - bo - dy, Yes, I do.
2. Love my mom - my, Yes, I do. Love my mom - my, Yes, I do.

Love some - bo - dy, Yes, I do. Love some - bo - dy but I won't say who.
Love my mom - my, Yes, I do. Love my mom-my Oh___ yes, I do.

Verses: Love my daddy. . . Love my sister. . . Love my brother. . . Love my Grandma . . .Love my Grandpa

A Tisket A Tasket

Children's Song

A tis - ket, a tas - ket, a green and yel - low bas - ket, I

wrote a let - ter to my love and on the way I lost it, I lost it, I lost it,

On the way I lost it, I wrote a let - ter to my love and on the way I lost it.

95

St. Patricks Day
Tune: Shoo Fly

Traditional
New Lyrics by Boyer

Come on, let's all wear green! Come on, let's all wear green.

Come on, let's all wear green 'cause it's St. Pa - trick's Day!

March Seventeen

Rene Boyer

March se - ven-teen, means wear-ing of the green. Be - cause it is St. Pa-trick's Day,

it has al - ways been that way; March sev - en-teen, means wear-in' of the green. St.

Pa-trick came from I - re-land, a coun-try cloaked in green, where sham-rocks dot the hill - sides, in

sum - mer and in spring. Le - pre-chauns, rain - bows, cas - tles old and gray,

Put them all to - ge - ther, It's St. Pa - trick's Day!

OUR FLAG

I see our country's colors
Wave red, white, and blue
On flags throughout our nation.
America, I love you!

I Love America
Tune: Skip to My Lou

Traditional
Lyrics: Rene Boyer

1. I love A-mer-i-ca, Yes, I do. I love A-mer-i-ca, Yes, I do.
2. I love A-mer-i-ca, Yes I do. I love A-mer-i-ca, Yes, I do.

I love A-mer-i-ca, Yes, I do. That's why I wear red, white and blue.
I kove A-mer-i-ca, Yes, I do. I love my flag's red, white and blue.

Battle Hymn of the Republic

William Steffe

Glo - ry, glo - ry hal - le - lu - jah! Glo - ry, glo - ry hal - le - lu - jah!
Glo - ry, glo - ry hal - le - lu - jah! His truth is march - ing on.

Yankee Doodle

Father and I Went Down to Camp

Traditional

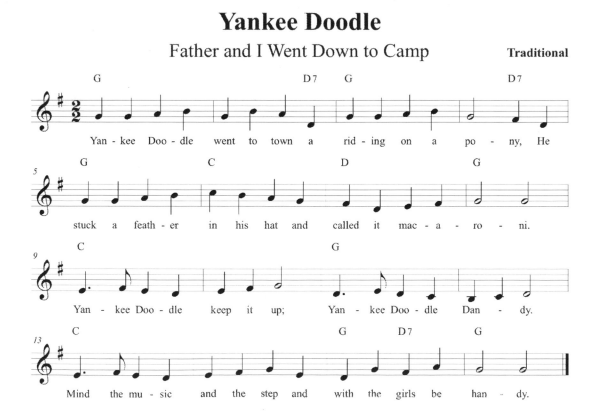

Yan - kee Doo - dle went to town a rid - ing on a po - ny, He
stuck a feath - er in his hat and called it mac - a - ro - ni.
Yan - kee Doo - dle keep it up; Yan - kee Doo - dle Dan - dy.
Mind the mu - sic and the step and with the girls be han - dy.

HALLOWEEN FUN

My jack-o'-lantern's carved and lit,
Ready for Halloween night
When ghosts and goblins roam the streets,
Causing such a fright!

A costume changes me into a
Princess or dinosaur,
Dragon, pirate, doctor, nurse,
Or a lion with a ferocious roar.

I carry a bag from house to house,
Collecting candy and things
While shouting out, "Trick or treat!"
What joy this Halloween brings!

When I go home and open my bag,
I marvel at the amount
Of pretzels, balloons, tattoos, and rings,
Too numerous for me to count!

My only wish is that this day
Could just go on till dawn.
But I know I can't make it
As I let out a great big yawn.

I'm A Little Snowman
Tune: I'm A Little Teapot

Traditional
New Lyrics by Boyer

I'm a lit-tle snow man, look at me. I am as hap-py as can be.

I have three black but-tons, scarf and hat, my eyes, my nose, and I'm round and fat.

MY SNOWMAN

I want to go out in the snow
To build a big snowman.
I'll need my hat, my coat, and boots
To carry out my plan.

I need to put on mittens.
The weather is very cold.
Also someone to help me
Roll two big snowballs.

Once the snowman's body
Is shaped up nice and round,
It'll be time to lift his head
From the frozen ground.
The head must sit directly
On top the snowman's bod,
For if it's not well balanced,
It will look quite odd.

For his eyes and smiling mouth,
I'll use black charcoal
To help him look kid-friendly.
I've a carrot for his nose.

I'll put a scarf around his neck.
Use sticks for arms and hands.
I'll need a hat to sit on top.
I know he'll look so grand!

Over the River and Through the Woods

Lydia Marie Child

O - ver the ri - ver and through the woods to grand - mo - ther's house we go. The horse knows the way to car - ry the sleigh through the white and drift - ed snow. O - ver the ri - ver and through the woods, Oh how the wind does blow. It stings the toes and bites the nose as o - ver the ground we go.

Jingle Bells

James Lord Pierpont
1822-1893

Jingle bells, jingle bells, Jingle all the way.

Oh, what fun it is to ride in a one horse o-pen sleigh, _____

Jingle bells, jingle bells, Jingle all the way.

Oh, what fun it is to ride in a one-horse o-pen sleigh.

I Have A Little Dreidel

Traditional

Toembai

Hebrew Folk Song

La Piñata

Mexican Folk Song

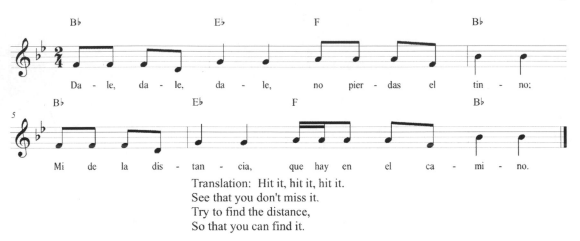

Da - le, da - le, da - le, no pier - das el tin - no;

Mi de la dis - tan - cia, que hay en el ca - mi - no.

Translation: Hit it, hit it, hit it.
See that you don't miss it.
Try to find the distance,
So that you can find it.

'Tis the Season
Tune: Deck the Hall

Traditional Carol
New Lyrics by Boyer

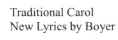

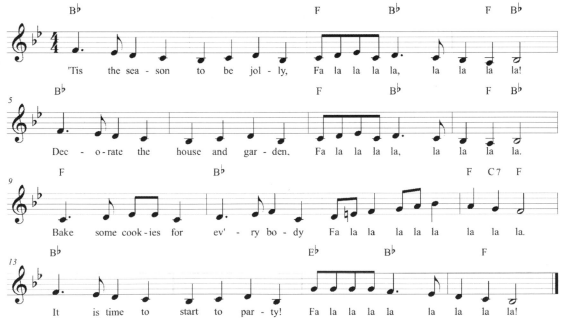

'Tis the sea - son to be jol - ly, Fa la la la la, la la la la!

Dec - o - rate the house and gar - den, Fa la la la la, la la la la.

Bake some cook - ies for ev' - ry bo - dy Fa la la la la la la la la.

It is time to start to par - ty! Fa la la la la la la la la!

Xin Nian Hao

Chinese New Year Song
Tune: Clementine

Traditional

Xin nian Hao - a, Xin nian Hao - a, Zhu he da - jia xin nian hao. Wo-men
Hap - py New Year, Hap - py New Year, Wish-ing all a spe - cial time, We are
(Shing neean how - a, Shing neean how - a, Jew he da jia shing nian how, Wo-man

chang - ge, wo men tiao wu, Zhu he da jia xin nian hao.
sing - ing, We are danc - ing, Wish-ing all, a spe - cial time
chang guah, Wo-man tiao oo, Jew he da jia shing nian how.)

We Want Peace

Tune: Ode to Joy

Beethoven
New Lyrics by Boyer

We want peace through - out our na - tion, We want peace through -

out our world. We want love and hap - pi - ness to

reign o'er lives of boys and girls. Lit - tle chil - dren

shar - ing and car - ing, for each oth - er ev' - ry day,

Liv - ing peace - ful - ly to - geth - er, while at work and while at play.

GOOD NIGHT

A bundle of kisses,
A bundle of hugs,
It's now time
To go to bed.

I'll hear a story.
Get tucked in tight.
It's time for me
To say, "Good night!"

Kum Ba Yah

Traditional

Kum-ba - yah my Lord, Kum-ba - yah. Kum-ba - yah my Lord, Kum-ba - yah. Kum-ba -

yah my Lord, Kum-ba - yah, Oh Lord,_____ Kum-ba - yah!

Are You Sleeping

Tune: Frere Jacques

Traditional French Folk Song

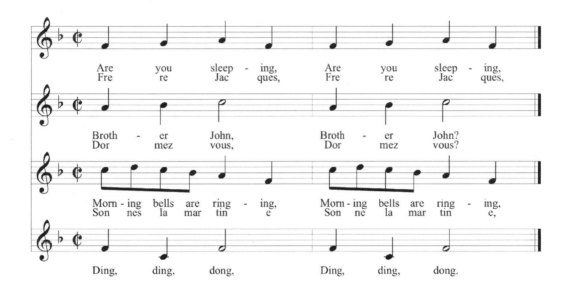

Are you sleep - ing,   Are you sleep - ing,
Fre   re   Jac   ques,   Fre   re   Jac   ques,

Broth - er   John,   Broth - er   John?
Dor   mez   vous,   Dor   mez   vous?

Morn - ing bells are ring - ing,   Morn - ing bells are ring - ing,
Son - nes   la   mar   tin   e   Son   ne   la   mar   tin   e,

Ding,   ding,   dong,   Ding,   ding,   dong.

Ten in the Bed

American Folk Song

1. There were ten in the bed, and the lit-tle one said, "Roll o - ver, roll o - ver!" So they
all rolled o - ver and one fell out!

Other Verses:

2. There were nine in the bed .. . . .
3. There were eight in the bed. . . .
4. There were seven in the bed. . . .
5. There were six in the bed.   . . .
6. There were five in the bed . . . .
7. There were four in the bed. . . .
8. There were three in the bed. . .
9. There were two in the bed, , , ,
10. There was one in the bed. . . . GOOD NIGHT

All the Pretty Little Horses

African American Lullaby

Hush-a-by, don't you cry, Go to sleep-y lit-tle ba - by. When you wake,
you shall have, all the pret-ty lit-tle hor - ses. Blacks and bays, dap-ples and grays,
all the pret-ty litt-le hor - ses. Hush-a - by, don't you cry, Go to sleep-y lit-tle ba - by.

Little Silver Moon

Chinese Folk Song

Lit-tle sil-ver moon float-ing high in the sky. Gent-ly pas-sing stars, as it floats, gent-ly by.

Sail, lit - tle moon boat, to the west. Sail, lit - tle moon boat, while I rest.

ABOUT RENÉ

René is a grandma who has served as a full-time nanny to grandchildren Caleb, Aurora, Margaux, and Phineas.

She is also a professor emerita of music education at the University of Cincinnati's College Conservatory of Music, where she worked as a music educator for over thirty years.

René is known nationally and internationally for her work in multicultural and urban music education. She is author of *Music Fundamentals, Methods and Materials for the Elementary Classroom Teacher*, published by Pearson, *Share the Music, Spotlight on Music, and Music Studio*, three K-8 basil textbook curriculum programs published by Macmillan McGraw-Hill, *Songs and Rhythms of a Nation, Expressions of Freedom: An Anthology of African American Spirituals* in three volumes, *Walking in the Light of Freedom*, also in three volumes, *The Ballad of the Underground Railroad* and *United We Stand*, published by Hal Leonard.

René received her BM and MM from Southern Illinois University in Edwardsville, Illinois, and her doctorate from Washington University in St. Louis, Missouri. She possesses all levels of Orff Certification as well as Kodaly Certification from Hungary.

René has received many awards for her contributions to music education, but her most coveted awards have come from her travels throughout the United States and abroad where she has been privileged to work with both children and teachers for the betterment of music in our schools.

Printed in the United States
By Bookmasters